50 Dreamy Dessert Recipes for Home

By: Kelly Johnson

Table of Contents

- Chocolate Lava Cake
- Tiramisu
- Lemon Meringue Pie
- Vanilla Bean Crème Brûlée
- Strawberry Shortcake
- Classic Cheesecake
- Chocolate Fondant
- Raspberry Macarons
- Red Velvet Cake
- Panna Cotta
- Bread Pudding
- Salted Caramel Brownies
- Key Lime Pie
- Blueberry Cheesecake Bars
- Almond Cake
- Apple Crisp
- Matcha Green Tea Cake
- Sticky Toffee Pudding
- Profiteroles
- Eclairs
- Lemon Bars
- Chocolate Chip Cookies
- Coconut Cream Pie
- Pumpkin Pie
- Churros
- Baklava
- Pecan Pie
- White Chocolate Raspberry Cheesecake
- Mocha Mousse
- Peanut Butter Pie
- Brown Butter Blondies
- Cherry Clafoutis
- Mango Sorbet
- Chocolate Truffles
- Pavlova
- Cinnamon Rolls

- Carrot Cake
- Raspberries and Cream Tart
- S'mores Bars
- Creme Caramel
- Apple Pie
- Pear Almond Tart
- Chocolate Soufflé
- Vanilla Pudding
- Strawberry Rhubarb Crisp
- Hazelnut Meringue Cake
- Key Lime Cheesecake
- Molten Chocolate Mug Cake
- Tiramisu Cupcakes
- Banana Foster

Chocolate Lava Cake

Ingredients:

- 1/2 cup unsalted butter (plus extra for greasing)
- 4 oz (115g) high-quality bittersweet chocolate, chopped
- 1 cup powdered sugar
- 2 large eggs
- 2 large egg yolks
- 1 tsp vanilla extract
- 1/2 cup all-purpose flour
- A pinch of salt
- Optional: ice cream or whipped cream for serving

Instructions:

1. **Preheat Oven**: Preheat your oven to 425°F (220°C). Grease four ramekins with butter and lightly dust them with cocoa powder or flour, tapping out the excess.
2. **Melt Butter and Chocolate**: In a microwave-safe bowl or using a double boiler, melt the butter and chopped chocolate together, stirring until smooth and combined. Let it cool slightly.
3. **Mix Dry Ingredients**: In a separate bowl, whisk together the powdered sugar, flour, and salt.
4. **Combine Wet Ingredients**: Add the eggs, egg yolks, and vanilla extract to the chocolate mixture, whisking until well combined.
5. **Combine Mixtures**: Gradually fold the dry ingredients into the chocolate mixture until just combined. Be careful not to overmix.
6. **Pour into Ramekins**: Divide the batter evenly among the prepared ramekins.
7. **Bake**: Place the ramekins on a baking sheet and bake for 12-14 minutes, or until the edges are set but the center is still soft and jiggly.
8. **Cool and Serve**: Let the cakes cool for 1 minute. Carefully run a knife around the edges of each cake to loosen them, then invert them onto plates. Serve immediately, ideally with a scoop of ice cream or a dollop of whipped cream.

Enjoy your delicious Chocolate Lava Cake!

Tiramisu

Ingredients:

- **For the Cream Mixture:**
    - 6 large egg yolks
    - 3/4 cup granulated sugar
    - 1 cup heavy cream
    - 8 oz (227g) mascarpone cheese, softened
    - 1 tsp vanilla extract
- **For the Coffee Mixture:**
    - 1 cup strong brewed coffee, cooled
    - 1/4 cup coffee liqueur (e.g., Marsala, Kahlua) – optional
- **For Assembly:**
    - 24-30 ladyfingers (savoiardi)
    - Unsweetened cocoa powder, for dusting
    - Grated chocolate or chocolate shavings (optional)

Instructions:

1. **Prepare Coffee Mixture**:
    - In a shallow dish, combine the cooled coffee and coffee liqueur (if using). Set aside.
2. **Make the Cream Mixture**:
    - In a medium heatproof bowl, whisk together the egg yolks and granulated sugar. Place the bowl over a pot of simmering water (double boiler) and cook, whisking constantly, for about 5 minutes, until the mixture is pale and thickened. Remove from heat and let it cool slightly.
    - In a separate bowl, whip the heavy cream until stiff peaks form.
    - Gently fold the mascarpone cheese and vanilla extract into the egg yolk mixture until smooth. Then fold in the whipped cream until fully combined.
3. **Assemble the Tiramisu**:
    - Briefly dip each ladyfinger into the coffee mixture, making sure not to soak them. Arrange a layer of dipped ladyfingers in the bottom of a 9x13-inch dish or individual serving glasses.
    - Spread half of the mascarpone cream mixture over the ladyfingers.
    - Add another layer of dipped ladyfingers on top of the cream.
    - Spread the remaining mascarpone cream mixture over the second layer of ladyfingers, smoothing the top.
4. **Chill**:
    - Cover and refrigerate the tiramisu for at least 4 hours, or overnight, to allow the flavors to meld and the dessert to firm up.
5. **Serve**:

- Before serving, dust the top with unsweetened cocoa powder and optionally sprinkle with grated chocolate or chocolate shavings.

Enjoy your homemade Tiramisu!

Lemon Meringue Pie

Ingredients:

For the Pie Crust:

- 1 1/2 cups all-purpose flour
- 1/2 cup unsalted butter (cold, cut into small pieces)
- 1/4 cup granulated sugar
- 1/4 tsp salt
- 2-3 tbsp ice water

For the Lemon Filling:

- 1 1/4 cups granulated sugar
- 1/4 cup cornstarch
- 1/4 tsp salt
- 1 1/2 cups water
- 3 large egg yolks
- 1/2 cup fresh lemon juice (about 2-3 lemons)
- 2 tbsp unsalted butter
- 1 tsp lemon zest

For the Meringue:

- 3 large egg whites
- 1/4 tsp cream of tartar
- 1/2 cup granulated sugar
- 1/2 tsp vanilla extract

Instructions:

1. Prepare the Pie Crust:

- In a large bowl, combine flour, sugar, and salt. Cut in the cold butter using a pastry cutter or your fingers until the mixture resembles coarse crumbs.
- Gradually add ice water, one tablespoon at a time, until the dough starts to come together. Do not overmix.
- Form the dough into a disk, wrap in plastic wrap, and refrigerate for at least 30 minutes.

2. Roll and Bake the Crust:

- Preheat your oven to 375°F (190°C).
- Roll out the chilled dough on a lightly floured surface to fit a 9-inch pie dish. Transfer the dough to the pie dish, trim the edges, and crimp them as desired.

- Line the pie crust with parchment paper or aluminum foil and fill with pie weights or dried beans. Bake for 15 minutes.
- Remove the weights and parchment/foil and bake for an additional 10 minutes, or until the crust is golden brown. Let it cool completely.

3. Make the Lemon Filling:

- In a medium saucepan, whisk together sugar, cornstarch, and salt. Gradually whisk in water.
- Cook over medium heat, stirring constantly, until the mixture comes to a boil and thickens (about 5-7 minutes).
- In a small bowl, lightly beat the egg yolks. Slowly whisk a small amount of the hot mixture into the egg yolks to temper them, then return the egg yolk mixture to the saucepan.
- Continue to cook for another 2 minutes, stirring constantly.
- Remove from heat and stir in lemon juice, butter, and lemon zest until the butter is melted and the mixture is smooth.
- Pour the lemon filling into the cooled pie crust.

4. Make the Meringue:

- In a large, clean bowl, beat the egg whites with cream of tartar until soft peaks form.
- Gradually add sugar, one tablespoon at a time, while continuing to beat until stiff, glossy peaks form.
- Beat in vanilla extract.

5. Assemble and Bake:

- Spread the meringue over the lemon filling, making sure to seal the edges to the crust to prevent shrinking.
- Use a spatula to create peaks and swirls in the meringue.
- Bake in the preheated oven at 350°F (175°C) for about 10-12 minutes, or until the meringue is golden brown.

6. Cool and Serve:

- Let the pie cool completely at room temperature before slicing, to allow the filling to set properly.

Enjoy your tangy and sweet Lemon Meringue Pie!

Vanilla Bean Crème Brûlée

Ingredients:

- **For the Custard:**
    - 2 cups heavy cream
    - 1 vanilla bean (or 2 tsp vanilla extract)
    - 5 large egg yolks
    - 1/2 cup granulated sugar
    - 1/4 cup brown sugar (for topping)

Instructions:

1. Preheat Oven:

- Preheat your oven to 325°F (163°C).

2. Prepare the Vanilla Bean:

- If using a vanilla bean, slice it lengthwise and scrape out the seeds. Add both the seeds and the bean pod to a medium saucepan with the heavy cream. If using vanilla extract, you'll add it later.

3. Heat the Cream:

- Heat the cream and vanilla bean over medium heat until just before it starts to boil. Remove from heat and let it steep for 10 minutes to infuse the vanilla flavor. If using vanilla extract, add it to the cream after it has steeped and before combining with the egg yolks.

4. Prepare the Custard Mixture:

- In a medium bowl, whisk together the egg yolks and granulated sugar until smooth and slightly pale.
- Slowly pour the hot cream mixture into the egg yolks, whisking constantly to temper the eggs and prevent curdling. Remove the vanilla bean pod if used.

5. Strain the Custard:

- Strain the custard through a fine-mesh sieve into a clean bowl or large measuring cup to remove any curdled bits or leftover vanilla bean particles.

6. Fill the Ramekins:

- Divide the custard mixture evenly among 4 to 6 ramekins (depending on size).

7. Bake in a Water Bath:

- Place the ramekins in a large baking dish or roasting pan. Pour hot water into the baking dish around the ramekins, making sure the water comes about halfway up the sides of the ramekins.
- Bake in the preheated oven for 30-40 minutes, or until the custards are set around the edges but still slightly jiggly in the center.

8. Cool and Chill:

- Remove the ramekins from the water bath and let them cool to room temperature. Refrigerate for at least 2 hours, or preferably overnight, to allow the custard to fully set and chill.

9. Caramelize the Sugar:

- Before serving, sprinkle an even layer of brown sugar over each custard. Use a kitchen torch to caramelize the sugar until it forms a crispy, golden-brown crust. If you don't have a torch, you can place the ramekins under a broiler set to high for 1-2 minutes, but watch closely to avoid burning.

10. Serve:

- Let the crème brûlée sit for a few minutes after caramelizing to allow the sugar to harden before serving.

Enjoy your rich and creamy Vanilla Bean Crème Brûlée!

Strawberry Shortcake

Ingredients:

For the Biscuits:

- 2 cups all-purpose flour
- 1/4 cup granulated sugar
- 1 tbsp baking powder
- 1/2 tsp salt
- 1/2 cup unsalted butter (cold, cut into small pieces)
- 3/4 cup whole milk (cold)

For the Strawberries:

- 1 pound fresh strawberries, hulled and sliced
- 1/4 cup granulated sugar

For the Whipped Cream:

- 1 cup heavy cream
- 2 tbsp powdered sugar
- 1 tsp vanilla extract

Instructions:

1. Prepare the Strawberries:

- In a medium bowl, toss the sliced strawberries with 1/4 cup of granulated sugar. Let them sit for at least 30 minutes to macerate and release their juices.

2. Make the Biscuits:

- Preheat your oven to 425°F (220°C).
- In a large bowl, whisk together flour, sugar, baking powder, and salt.
- Cut in the cold butter using a pastry cutter or your fingers until the mixture resembles coarse crumbs.
- Pour in the cold milk and stir until just combined. The dough will be slightly sticky.
- Turn the dough out onto a floured surface and gently pat it into a 1-inch thick rectangle. Fold the dough over itself a few times to create layers, then gently roll it out to about 1-inch thickness.
- Cut the dough into 6-8 circles using a biscuit cutter or a round glass.
- Place the biscuits on a baking sheet lined with parchment paper. Bake for 12-15 minutes, or until the biscuits are golden brown. Let them cool slightly.

3. Whip the Cream:

- In a chilled mixing bowl, beat the heavy cream with an electric mixer until it starts to thicken.
- Add powdered sugar and vanilla extract. Continue beating until stiff peaks form.

4. Assemble the Shortcakes:

- Slice each biscuit in half horizontally. Place the bottom half on serving plates.
- Spoon a generous amount of macerated strawberries over the biscuit bottoms, including some of the juices.
- Top with a dollop of whipped cream.
- Place the biscuit tops on the whipped cream and add a little more whipped cream and strawberries on top.

5. Serve:

- Serve the Strawberry Shortcakes immediately, while the biscuits are still slightly warm.

Enjoy your delightful Strawberry Shortcake!

Classic Cheesecake

Ingredients:

For the Crust:

- 1 1/2 cups graham cracker crumbs
- 1/4 cup granulated sugar
- 1/2 cup unsalted butter (melted)

For the Filling:

- 4 (8 oz each) packages cream cheese (room temperature)
- 1 cup granulated sugar
- 1 tsp vanilla extract
- 4 large eggs
- 1 cup sour cream
- 1 cup heavy cream

For the Topping (Optional):

- Fresh berries or fruit sauce
- Whipped cream

Instructions:

1. Preheat Oven:

- Preheat your oven to 325°F (163°C).

2. Prepare the Crust:

- In a medium bowl, combine the graham cracker crumbs, granulated sugar, and melted butter. Mix until the crumbs are evenly coated.
- Press the mixture firmly into the bottom of a 9-inch springform pan to form an even layer.
- Bake for 10 minutes, then remove from the oven and let it cool slightly.

3. Prepare the Filling:

- In a large bowl, beat the cream cheese with an electric mixer on medium speed until smooth and creamy.
- Gradually add the granulated sugar, beating until fully combined.
- Beat in the vanilla extract.
- Add the eggs, one at a time, beating on low speed after each addition until just combined. Avoid overmixing.
- Mix in the sour cream and heavy cream until smooth and well combined.

4. Bake the Cheesecake:

- Pour the cream cheese filling over the cooled crust in the springform pan.
- Smooth the top with a spatula.
- Bake in the preheated oven for 50-60 minutes, or until the edges are set but the center is still slightly jiggly. A knife or toothpick inserted into the center should come out mostly clean.
- Turn off the oven and crack the oven door slightly. Let the cheesecake cool in the oven for 1 hour. This helps prevent cracks.

5. Chill the Cheesecake:

- After cooling in the oven, remove the cheesecake from the oven and refrigerate for at least 4 hours, or preferably overnight, to allow it to fully set.

6. Add Toppings and Serve:

- Before serving, top the cheesecake with fresh berries, fruit sauce, or whipped cream if desired.
- Run a knife around the edges of the cheesecake to help release it from the springform pan, then remove the sides of the pan.

Enjoy your delicious, classic cheesecake!

Chocolate Fondant

Ingredients:

- **For the Fondant:**
    - 1/2 cup (1 stick) unsalted butter (plus extra for greasing)
    - 4 oz (115g) high-quality bittersweet or semisweet chocolate, chopped
    - 1 cup powdered sugar
    - 2 large eggs
    - 2 large egg yolks
    - 1 tsp vanilla extract
    - 1/2 cup all-purpose flour
    - A pinch of salt
- **For Serving (Optional):**
    - Vanilla ice cream or whipped cream
    - Fresh berries

Instructions:

1. Preheat Oven:

- Preheat your oven to 425°F (220°C).

2. Prepare the Ramekins:

- Grease four ramekins (or custard cups) generously with butter. You can also dust them lightly with cocoa powder or flour, tapping out the excess.

3. Melt Butter and Chocolate:

- In a microwave-safe bowl or using a double boiler, melt the butter and chopped chocolate together, stirring until smooth and combined. Let it cool slightly.

4. Mix Dry Ingredients:

- In a separate bowl, whisk together the powdered sugar, flour, and salt.

5. Combine Wet Ingredients:

- Add the eggs, egg yolks, and vanilla extract to the chocolate mixture, whisking until fully incorporated.

6. Fold in Dry Ingredients:

- Gradually fold the dry ingredients into the chocolate mixture until just combined. Be careful not to overmix.

7. Fill the Ramekins:

- Divide the batter evenly among the prepared ramekins.

8. Bake:

- Place the ramekins on a baking sheet and bake in the preheated oven for 12-14 minutes. The edges should be set, but the center should still be soft and jiggly.

9. Cool and Serve:

- Let the cakes cool for 1 minute. Carefully run a knife around the edges to loosen them, then invert each ramekin onto a plate.
- Serve immediately with a scoop of vanilla ice cream or a dollop of whipped cream, and fresh berries if desired.

Enjoy your decadent Chocolate Fondant!

Raspberry Macarons

Ingredients:

For the Macaron Shells:

- 1 1/2 cups (150g) almond flour
- 1 1/2 cups (180g) powdered sugar
- 1/2 cup (120g) egg whites (about 4 large eggs)
- 1/4 cup (50g) granulated sugar
- 1/2 tsp vanilla extract
- 1/4 tsp cream of tartar (optional)
- Red or pink gel food coloring (optional)

For the Raspberry Filling:

- 1/2 cup (115g) unsalted butter (softened)
- 1 1/2 cups (190g) powdered sugar
- 1/4 cup (60g) raspberry jam or raspberry puree
- 1/2 tsp vanilla extract

Instructions:

1. Prepare Baking Sheets:

- Preheat your oven to 300°F (150°C). Line two baking sheets with parchment paper or silicone baking mats.

2. Prepare Dry Ingredients:

- In a medium bowl, sift together the almond flour and powdered sugar. This ensures a smooth texture for the macaron shells.

3. Make the Meringue:

- In a clean, dry bowl, beat the egg whites with an electric mixer on medium speed until foamy. If using, add the cream of tartar.
- Gradually add the granulated sugar while continuing to beat on high speed until stiff, glossy peaks form. If using food coloring, add it during this step and beat until the color is evenly distributed.

4. Combine Ingredients:

- Gently fold the sifted almond flour mixture into the meringue in three additions. Use a spatula and fold until the mixture flows like lava and forms a figure-eight pattern when dropped from the spatula.

5. Pipe the Macarons:

- Transfer the macaron batter to a piping bag fitted with a round tip (about 1/2 inch in diameter). Pipe small circles (about 1.5 inches in diameter) onto the prepared baking sheets, spacing them about 1 inch apart.
- Tap the baking sheets firmly on the counter to release any air bubbles and smooth the tops of the macarons.

6. Rest the Macarons:

- Let the piped macarons sit at room temperature for 30-60 minutes, or until a skin forms on the surface. This helps them develop the characteristic "feet" when baked.

7. Bake:

- Bake in the preheated oven for 15-18 minutes, or until the macarons have risen and are firm to the touch. Rotate the baking sheets halfway through baking to ensure even cooking.

8. Cool and Fill:

- Let the macarons cool completely on the baking sheets before removing them.
- For the filling, beat together the softened butter and powdered sugar until creamy. Mix in the raspberry jam or puree and vanilla extract until well combined.

9. Assemble:

- Pipe a small amount of raspberry filling onto the flat side of one macaron shell. Top with another shell to form a sandwich. Gently press together to spread the filling evenly.

10. Rest and Serve:

- For best results, let the assembled macarons rest in the refrigerator for 24 hours before serving. This allows the flavors to meld and the filling to soften the shells slightly.

Enjoy your beautiful and delicious Raspberry Macarons!

Red Velvet Cake

Ingredients:

For the Cake:

- 2 1/2 cups (315g) all-purpose flour
- 1 1/2 cups (300g) granulated sugar
- 1 tsp baking soda
- 1/2 tsp baking powder
- 1/2 tsp salt
- 1 cup (240ml) vegetable oil
- 1 cup (240ml) buttermilk (room temperature)
- 2 large eggs
- 2 tbsp red food coloring (gel or liquid)
- 1 tbsp cocoa powder
- 1 tsp vanilla extract
- 1 tsp white vinegar

For the Cream Cheese Frosting:

- 8 oz (227g) cream cheese (softened)
- 1/2 cup (115g) unsalted butter (softened)
- 4 cups (480g) powdered sugar
- 1 tsp vanilla extract

Instructions:

1. Preheat Oven:

- Preheat your oven to 350°F (175°C). Grease and flour two 9-inch round cake pans (or line them with parchment paper).

2. Prepare Dry Ingredients:

- In a large bowl, sift together the flour, sugar, baking soda, baking powder, and salt.

3. Combine Wet Ingredients:

- In a separate bowl, whisk together the oil, buttermilk, eggs, food coloring, cocoa powder, vanilla extract, and vinegar until well combined.

4. Mix the Batter:

- Gradually add the wet ingredients to the dry ingredients, mixing just until combined. Be careful not to overmix.

5. Bake:

- Divide the batter evenly between the prepared cake pans. Smooth the tops with a spatula.
- Bake in the preheated oven for 25-30 minutes, or until a toothpick inserted into the center comes out clean.
- Allow the cakes to cool in the pans for 10 minutes, then transfer to a wire rack to cool completely.

6. Prepare the Cream Cheese Frosting:

- In a large bowl, beat the softened cream cheese and butter together until smooth and creamy.
- Gradually add the powdered sugar, beating on low speed until combined. Increase speed and beat until fluffy.
- Mix in the vanilla extract.

7. Frost the Cake:

- If the cakes have domed tops, level them with a knife or cake leveler.
- Place one cake layer on a serving plate or cake stand. Spread a layer of cream cheese frosting on top.
- Place the second cake layer on top and spread frosting over the top and sides of the cake.
- Decorate as desired with additional frosting, sprinkles, or decorations.

8. Chill and Serve:

- Refrigerate the cake for at least 30 minutes before serving to allow the frosting to set.

Enjoy your beautiful and delicious Red Velvet Cake!

Panna Cotta

Ingredients:

For the Panna Cotta:

- 1 cup whole milk
- 1 cup heavy cream
- 1/2 cup granulated sugar
- 1 tsp vanilla extract (or 1 vanilla bean, split and seeds scraped)
- 2 1/2 tsp unflavored gelatin powder (about 1 packet)
- 3 tbsp cold water (for blooming gelatin)

For the Berry Compote (Optional):

- 1 cup mixed berries (fresh or frozen)
- 1/4 cup granulated sugar
- 1 tbsp lemon juice

Instructions:

1. Prepare the Gelatin:

- In a small bowl, sprinkle the gelatin over the cold water. Let it sit for about 5 minutes to bloom.

2. Heat the Cream Mixture:

- In a medium saucepan, combine the milk, heavy cream, and granulated sugar. If using a vanilla bean, add the bean and seeds to the saucepan.
- Heat the mixture over medium heat, stirring occasionally, until the sugar is dissolved and the mixture is hot but not boiling. Remove from heat.

3. Dissolve the Gelatin:

- Add the bloomed gelatin to the hot cream mixture and stir until completely dissolved. If you used a vanilla bean, remove the bean pod now.

4. Add Vanilla Extract:

- Stir in the vanilla extract if you used vanilla extract instead of a vanilla bean.

5. Pour and Chill:

- Pour the mixture into ramekins, glasses, or molds of your choice.
- Refrigerate for at least 4 hours, or until set. For best results, chill overnight.

6. Prepare the Berry Compote (Optional):

- In a small saucepan, combine the mixed berries, granulated sugar, and lemon juice.
- Cook over medium heat, stirring occasionally, until the berries are softened and the mixture has thickened slightly, about 10-15 minutes.
- Let the compote cool to room temperature.

7. Serve:

- To serve, run a knife around the edges of the panna cotta and carefully unmold it onto serving plates, or serve it directly from the ramekins.
- Spoon the berry compote over the panna cotta just before serving.

Enjoy your creamy and elegant Panna Cotta with a fresh berry topping!

Bread Pudding

Ingredients:

For the Bread Pudding:

- 6 cups stale bread (cubed, about 1-inch pieces) – you can use French bread, challah, or brioche
- 2 cups whole milk
- 1 cup heavy cream
- 3/4 cup granulated sugar
- 4 large eggs
- 1 tsp vanilla extract
- 1 tsp ground cinnamon
- 1/4 tsp ground nutmeg
- 1/2 cup raisins or dried fruit (optional)
- 1/2 cup chopped nuts (optional)

For the Sauce (Optional):

- 1/2 cup butter
- 1 cup powdered sugar
- 1/4 cup milk
- 1/2 tsp vanilla extract

Instructions:

1. Preheat Oven:

- Preheat your oven to 350°F (175°C). Grease a 9x13-inch baking dish or a similar-sized dish.

2. Prepare the Bread:

- Place the cubed bread in a large bowl. If the bread isn't stale, you can toast it lightly in the oven to dry it out a bit.

3. Make the Custard Mixture:

- In a medium saucepan, combine the milk and heavy cream. Heat over medium heat until hot but not boiling. Remove from heat.
- In a large bowl, whisk together the sugar, eggs, vanilla extract, cinnamon, and nutmeg. Gradually whisk in the hot milk mixture until well combined.

4. Combine Bread and Custard:

- Pour the custard mixture over the bread cubes. Gently fold to coat the bread evenly. Let it sit for about 15-20 minutes to allow the bread to soak up the custard.

5. Add Optional Ingredients:

- If using, stir in the raisins or dried fruit and chopped nuts.

6. Bake:

- Pour the bread mixture into the prepared baking dish. Spread it out evenly.
- Bake in the preheated oven for 45-55 minutes, or until the top is golden brown and the pudding is set in the center (a knife inserted into the center should come out clean).

7. Make the Sauce (Optional):

- While the pudding is baking, prepare the sauce if desired.
- In a small saucepan, melt the butter over medium heat. Stir in the powdered sugar, milk, and vanilla extract. Cook, stirring constantly, until smooth and heated through.

8. Serve:

- Let the bread pudding cool slightly before serving. Drizzle with the optional sauce if desired, or serve with a scoop of vanilla ice cream or a dollop of whipped cream.

Enjoy your warm, comforting Bread Pudding!

Salted Caramel Brownies

Ingredients:

For the Brownies:

- 1 cup (2 sticks) unsalted butter
- 8 oz (225g) semisweet or bittersweet chocolate, chopped
- 1 1/4 cups granulated sugar
- 1/2 cup packed brown sugar
- 4 large eggs
- 1 tsp vanilla extract
- 1 cup all-purpose flour
- 1/4 tsp salt

For the Salted Caramel Sauce:

- 1 cup granulated sugar
- 6 tbsp unsalted butter, cut into pieces
- 1/2 cup heavy cream
- 1/2 tsp sea salt (or to taste)

Instructions:

1. Prepare the Brownies:

- Preheat your oven to 350°F (175°C). Grease and line a 9x13-inch baking pan with parchment paper, leaving an overhang for easy removal.
- In a medium saucepan, melt the butter over medium heat. Add the chopped chocolate and stir until fully melted and smooth. Remove from heat and let it cool slightly.
- Stir in the granulated sugar and brown sugar until combined.
- Add the eggs one at a time, mixing well after each addition. Stir in the vanilla extract.
- Fold in the flour and salt until just combined. Be careful not to overmix.
- Pour the brownie batter into the prepared pan and spread it evenly.

2. Make the Salted Caramel Sauce:

- In a medium saucepan over medium heat, melt the granulated sugar, stirring constantly with a wooden spoon or heat-resistant spatula. The sugar will clump up before eventually melting into a smooth, amber-colored liquid.
- Once the sugar is fully melted, carefully add the butter. The mixture will bubble vigorously. Stir until the butter is completely melted and combined.
- Slowly pour in the heavy cream while continuing to stir. The mixture will bubble again. Stir until smooth and combined.
- Remove from heat and stir in the sea salt. Let the caramel sauce cool slightly.

3. Assemble and Bake:

- Pour about half of the caramel sauce over the brownie batter, drizzling it in random spots. Use a knife or skewer to swirl the caramel into the batter, creating a marbled effect.
- Bake in the preheated oven for 25-30 minutes, or until a toothpick inserted into the center comes out mostly clean with a few moist crumbs. The brownies should be set but fudgy in the center.

4. Add More Caramel:

- Once the brownies are done baking, remove them from the oven and immediately drizzle the remaining caramel sauce over the top. Sprinkle with a little extra sea salt if desired.
- Allow the brownies to cool completely in the pan on a wire rack before cutting into squares.

Enjoy your indulgent Salted Caramel Brownies!

Key Lime Pie

Ingredients:

For the Crust:

- 1 1/2 cups graham cracker crumbs
- 1/4 cup granulated sugar
- 1/2 cup unsalted butter (melted)

For the Filling:

- 1 can (14 oz) sweetened condensed milk
- 1/2 cup sour cream
- 1/2 cup key lime juice (fresh or bottled)
- 3 large egg yolks
- 1 tsp lime zest (optional, for extra flavor)

For the Topping (Optional):

- 1 cup heavy cream
- 2 tbsp powdered sugar
- 1/2 tsp vanilla extract
- Lime wedges or additional lime zest for garnish

Instructions:

1. Preheat Oven:

- Preheat your oven to 350°F (175°C).

2. Prepare the Crust:

- In a medium bowl, combine the graham cracker crumbs, granulated sugar, and melted butter. Mix until the crumbs are evenly coated and the mixture resembles wet sand.
- Press the mixture firmly into the bottom and up the sides of a 9-inch pie dish to form an even layer. Use the back of a spoon or the bottom of a glass to press it down firmly.
- Bake the crust in the preheated oven for 8-10 minutes, or until lightly golden. Remove from the oven and let it cool while you prepare the filling.

3. Prepare the Filling:

- In a large bowl, whisk together the sweetened condensed milk, sour cream, key lime juice, and lime zest (if using) until smooth and well combined.
- Add the egg yolks and whisk until fully incorporated.

4. Bake the Pie:

- Pour the filling into the cooled graham cracker crust and spread it evenly.
- Bake in the preheated oven for 15-20 minutes, or until the filling is set and slightly jiggly in the center. The edges should be firm but the center should still have a slight wobble.
- Turn off the oven and let the pie cool in the oven with the door slightly open for about 1 hour. This helps prevent cracking.

5. Chill:

- Refrigerate the pie for at least 4 hours, or preferably overnight, to allow the filling to set and the flavors to meld.

6. Prepare the Topping (Optional):

- In a medium bowl, beat the heavy cream with an electric mixer until soft peaks form.
- Add the powdered sugar and vanilla extract. Continue beating until stiff peaks form.

7. Serve:

- Spread or pipe the whipped cream over the chilled pie. Garnish with lime wedges or additional lime zest if desired.

Enjoy your refreshing and tangy Key Lime Pie!

Blueberry Cheesecake Bars

Ingredients:

For the Crust:

- 1 1/2 cups graham cracker crumbs
- 1/4 cup granulated sugar
- 1/2 cup unsalted butter (melted)

For the Cheesecake Filling:

- 16 oz (450g) cream cheese (softened)
- 1/2 cup granulated sugar
- 1/2 cup sour cream
- 2 large eggs
- 1 tsp vanilla extract

For the Blueberry Topping:

- 2 cups fresh or frozen blueberries
- 1/2 cup granulated sugar
- 1 tbsp lemon juice
- 1 tbsp cornstarch
- 1/4 cup water

Instructions:

1. Preheat Oven:

- Preheat your oven to 325°F (163°C). Line an 8x8-inch or 9x9-inch baking pan with parchment paper, leaving an overhang for easy removal.

2. Prepare the Crust:

- In a medium bowl, combine the graham cracker crumbs, granulated sugar, and melted butter. Mix until the crumbs are evenly coated and the mixture resembles wet sand.
- Press the mixture firmly into the bottom of the prepared baking pan to form an even layer.
- Bake in the preheated oven for 8-10 minutes, or until slightly golden. Remove from the oven and let it cool slightly.

3. Prepare the Cheesecake Filling:

- In a large bowl, beat the softened cream cheese and granulated sugar until smooth and creamy.

- Add the sour cream and beat until fully combined.
- Beat in the eggs one at a time, mixing well after each addition. Stir in the vanilla extract.
- Pour the cream cheese mixture over the cooled graham cracker crust and smooth the top with a spatula.

4. Bake the Cheesecake Bars:

- Bake in the preheated oven for 30-35 minutes, or until the center is set and the edges are slightly puffed. The center should be slightly jiggly.
- Turn off the oven and let the bars cool in the oven with the door slightly ajar for 1 hour. This helps prevent cracking.

5. Prepare the Blueberry Topping:

- In a medium saucepan, combine the blueberries, granulated sugar, and lemon juice. Cook over medium heat until the blueberries release their juices and the mixture starts to simmer.
- In a small bowl, mix the cornstarch with water to create a slurry. Add this slurry to the blueberry mixture, stirring constantly until the sauce thickens and becomes glossy.
- Remove from heat and let it cool slightly.

6. Assemble and Chill:

- Spread the blueberry topping evenly over the cooled cheesecake layer.
- Refrigerate the bars for at least 4 hours, or overnight, to allow the filling to set completely and the flavors to meld.

7. Serve:

- Once fully chilled and set, lift the bars out of the pan using the parchment paper overhang. Cut into squares and serve.

Enjoy your delightful Blueberry Cheesecake Bars!

Almond Cake

Ingredients:

For the Cake:

- 1 cup (226g) unsalted butter (room temperature)
- 1 cup (200g) granulated sugar
- 4 large eggs
- 1 cup (120g) almond flour (or finely ground almonds)
- 1 cup (120g) all-purpose flour
- 1 tsp baking powder
- 1/2 tsp salt
- 1 tsp vanilla extract
- 1/2 tsp almond extract
- 1/2 cup (120ml) milk (whole or buttermilk)

For the Glaze (Optional):

- 1 cup (120g) powdered sugar
- 2-3 tbsp milk (or almond milk)
- 1/4 tsp almond extract

For Garnish (Optional):

- Sliced almonds
- Fresh berries

Instructions:

1. Preheat Oven:

- Preheat your oven to 350°F (175°C). Grease and flour a 9-inch round cake pan or line it with parchment paper.

2. Cream the Butter and Sugar:

- In a large bowl, beat the butter and granulated sugar together with an electric mixer until light and fluffy, about 3-4 minutes.

3. Add the Eggs:

- Add the eggs one at a time, beating well after each addition. Mix in the vanilla and almond extracts.

4. Combine Dry Ingredients:

- In a separate bowl, whisk together the almond flour, all-purpose flour, baking powder, and salt.

5. **Mix Dry and Wet Ingredients:**

    - Gradually add the dry ingredients to the butter mixture, alternating with the milk, beginning and ending with the dry ingredients. Mix until just combined.

6. **Bake the Cake:**

    - Pour the batter into the prepared cake pan and smooth the top with a spatula.
    - Bake in the preheated oven for 30-35 minutes, or until a toothpick inserted into the center comes out clean and the cake is golden brown.
    - Allow the cake to cool in the pan for 10 minutes before transferring to a wire rack to cool completely.

7. **Prepare the Glaze (Optional):**

    - In a small bowl, whisk together the powdered sugar, milk, and almond extract until smooth and pourable.
    - Drizzle the glaze over the cooled cake.

8. **Garnish and Serve:**

    - If desired, sprinkle the cake with sliced almonds and top with fresh berries before serving.

Enjoy your delightful Almond Cake, perfect for any occasion!

Apple Crisp

Ingredients:

For the Apple Filling:

- 6 cups peeled, cored, and sliced apples (about 4-5 medium apples; Granny Smith, Honeycrisp, or a mix works well)
- 1/2 cup granulated sugar
- 1/4 cup packed brown sugar
- 1 tbsp lemon juice
- 1 tsp ground cinnamon
- 1/4 tsp ground nutmeg
- 1/4 tsp salt
- 2 tbsp all-purpose flour (to thicken)

For the Crisp Topping:

- 3/4 cup old-fashioned rolled oats
- 1/2 cup all-purpose flour
- 1/2 cup packed brown sugar
- 1/4 cup granulated sugar
- 1/2 tsp ground cinnamon
- 1/4 tsp salt
- 1/2 cup unsalted butter (cold and cut into small pieces)

Instructions:

1. Preheat Oven:

- Preheat your oven to 350°F (175°C). Grease a 9x13-inch baking dish or a similar-sized dish.

2. Prepare the Apple Filling:

- In a large bowl, combine the sliced apples with granulated sugar, brown sugar, lemon juice, ground cinnamon, nutmeg, salt, and flour. Toss until the apples are evenly coated.
- Transfer the apple mixture to the prepared baking dish, spreading it out evenly.

3. Prepare the Crisp Topping:

- In a medium bowl, combine the rolled oats, flour, brown sugar, granulated sugar, ground cinnamon, and salt.
- Add the cold butter pieces and use a pastry cutter or your fingers to work the butter into the dry ingredients until the mixture resembles coarse crumbs.

4. Assemble and Bake:

- Sprinkle the crisp topping evenly over the apple filling.
- Bake in the preheated oven for 45-55 minutes, or until the topping is golden brown and the apple filling is bubbling and tender.

5. Serve:

- Let the apple crisp cool slightly before serving. It can be enjoyed warm or at room temperature.
- For an extra treat, serve with a scoop of vanilla ice cream or a dollop of whipped cream.

Enjoy your delicious and comforting Apple Crisp!

Matcha Green Tea Cake

Ingredients:

For the Cake:

- 1 1/2 cups (190g) all-purpose flour
- 1 cup (200g) granulated sugar
- 1/4 cup (50g) vegetable oil
- 1/2 cup (120ml) whole milk
- 3 large eggs
- 2 tbsp matcha green tea powder (culinary grade)
- 2 tsp baking powder
- 1/4 tsp salt
- 1 tsp vanilla extract

For the Matcha Glaze (Optional):

- 1 cup (120g) powdered sugar
- 2-3 tbsp milk (or almond milk)
- 1-2 tsp matcha green tea powder

Instructions:

1. Preheat Oven:

- Preheat your oven to 350°F (175°C). Grease and flour an 8-inch round cake pan or line it with parchment paper.

2. Prepare the Cake Batter:

- In a medium bowl, whisk together the flour, baking powder, salt, and matcha green tea powder. Set aside.
- In a large bowl, beat the granulated sugar and vegetable oil together until combined.
- Add the eggs one at a time, beating well after each addition.
- Stir in the vanilla extract.
- Gradually add the dry ingredients to the wet ingredients, alternating with the milk, beginning and ending with the dry ingredients. Mix until just combined.

3. Bake the Cake:

- Pour the batter into the prepared cake pan and smooth the top with a spatula.
- Bake in the preheated oven for 25-30 minutes, or until a toothpick inserted into the center comes out clean.
- Allow the cake to cool in the pan for 10 minutes before transferring it to a wire rack to cool completely.

4. Prepare the Matcha Glaze (Optional):

- In a small bowl, whisk together the powdered sugar and matcha green tea powder.
- Gradually add milk, a little at a time, until the glaze reaches a pourable consistency.
- Drizzle the glaze over the cooled cake.

5. Serve:

- Once the glaze has set, the cake is ready to be served. You can also garnish with additional matcha powder or fresh berries if desired.

Enjoy your elegant and flavorful Matcha Green Tea Cake!

Sticky Toffee Pudding

Ingredients:

For the Pudding:

- 1 cup (150g) chopped dates (pitted)
- 1 cup (240ml) boiling water
- 1 tsp baking soda
- 1/2 cup (115g) unsalted butter (room temperature)
- 1/2 cup (100g) granulated sugar
- 1/4 cup (50g) packed brown sugar
- 2 large eggs
- 1 tsp vanilla extract
- 1 1/2 cups (190g) all-purpose flour
- 1 tsp baking powder
- 1/4 tsp salt

For the Toffee Sauce:

- 1/2 cup (115g) unsalted butter
- 1 cup (200g) packed brown sugar
- 1/2 cup (120ml) heavy cream
- 1/2 tsp vanilla extract

Instructions:

1. Preheat Oven:

- Preheat your oven to 350°F (175°C). Grease a 9x9-inch baking dish or a similar-sized dish.

2. Prepare the Dates:

- In a bowl, combine the chopped dates and baking soda. Pour the boiling water over the dates and stir. Let it sit for about 10 minutes until the dates are softened.

3. Make the Pudding Batter:

- In a large bowl, cream together the butter, granulated sugar, and brown sugar until light and fluffy.
- Beat in the eggs one at a time, followed by the vanilla extract.
- In a separate bowl, whisk together the flour, baking powder, and salt.
- Gradually add the dry ingredients to the butter mixture, mixing just until combined.
- Stir in the date mixture (including any liquid) until fully incorporated.

4. Bake the Pudding:

- Pour the batter into the prepared baking dish and smooth the top.
- Bake in the preheated oven for 30-35 minutes, or until a toothpick inserted into the center comes out clean.

5. Prepare the Toffee Sauce:

- In a medium saucepan, melt the butter over medium heat.
- Stir in the brown sugar and cook, stirring constantly, until the sugar is fully dissolved and the mixture starts to bubble.
- Gradually stir in the heavy cream and continue to cook for another 2-3 minutes, until the sauce is smooth and thickened.
- Remove from heat and stir in the vanilla extract.

6. Serve:

- Once the pudding is baked, allow it to cool for a few minutes before serving.
- Cut the pudding into squares and serve warm with a generous drizzle of toffee sauce on top.

For an extra treat, you can serve the sticky toffee pudding with a scoop of vanilla ice cream or a dollop of whipped cream.

Enjoy your delicious and comforting Sticky Toffee Pudding!

Profiteroles

Ingredients

For the Choux Pastry:

- **1/2 cup (115g) butter**, cut into pieces
- **1 cup (240ml) water**
- **1 cup (125g) all-purpose flour**
- **4 large eggs**
- **1/4 teaspoon salt**

For the Filling (Pastry Cream or Whipped Cream):

- **1 cup (240ml) heavy cream** (for whipped cream) or **2 cups (480ml) milk** (for pastry cream)
- **2 tablespoons sugar**
- **1 teaspoon vanilla extract**

For Pastry Cream:

- **3 large egg yolks**
- **1/4 cup (50g) sugar**
- **2 tablespoons cornstarch**
- **1 tablespoon butter**

For the Chocolate Sauce:

- **1/2 cup (120ml) heavy cream**
- **1 cup (175g) semi-sweet chocolate chips**

Instructions

1. Make the Choux Pastry:

1. Preheat your oven to 400°F (200°C). Line a baking sheet with parchment paper.
2. In a medium saucepan, combine the butter, water, and salt. Heat over medium heat until the butter is melted and the mixture begins to boil.
3. Remove from heat and add the flour all at once. Stir vigorously with a wooden spoon until the mixture pulls away from the sides of the pan and forms a smooth ball.
4. Return the pan to medium heat and cook for about 1-2 minutes, stirring constantly, to dry out the dough slightly.
5. Transfer the dough to a mixing bowl and let it cool for a few minutes. Beat in the eggs one at a time, making sure each egg is fully incorporated before adding the next. The dough should be smooth and glossy.

6. Using a pastry bag fitted with a plain round tip or a spoon, pipe small mounds (about 1-inch in diameter) onto the prepared baking sheet.
7. Bake for 20-25 minutes or until the puffs are golden brown and crisp. Do not open the oven door while baking. Let the profiteroles cool completely on a wire rack.

2. Prepare the Filling:

For Whipped Cream:

1. In a large mixing bowl, beat the heavy cream and sugar with an electric mixer until stiff peaks form. Add vanilla extract and mix until combined.

For Pastry Cream:

1. In a medium saucepan, heat the milk until it's just about to boil. Remove from heat.
2. In a bowl, whisk together the egg yolks, sugar, and cornstarch until pale and thick.
3. Gradually whisk the hot milk into the egg mixture.
4. Return the mixture to the saucepan and cook over medium heat, whisking constantly, until thickened and just starting to boil.
5. Remove from heat and whisk in the butter and vanilla extract. Transfer to a bowl, cover with plastic wrap (pressing it directly onto the surface to prevent a skin from forming), and let it cool to room temperature.

3. Prepare the Chocolate Sauce:

1. In a small saucepan, heat the heavy cream over medium heat until it just begins to simmer.
2. Remove from heat and add the chocolate chips. Let them sit for a minute, then stir until the chocolate is completely melted and the sauce is smooth.

4. Assemble the Profiteroles:

1. Once the profiteroles are cooled, cut a small slit in the side of each to create an opening.
2. Fill each profiterole with whipped cream or pastry cream using a pastry bag fitted with a small tip or a spoon.
3. Drizzle or dip the filled profiteroles with the warm chocolate sauce.

Enjoy your homemade profiteroles! They're best served the day they're made but can be stored in an airtight container for a short period.

Eclairs

Ingredients

For the Choux Pastry:

- **1/2 cup (115g) butter**, cut into pieces
- **1 cup (240ml) water**
- **1 cup (125g) all-purpose flour**
- **4 large eggs**
- **1/4 teaspoon salt**

For the Filling:

- **2 cups (480ml) milk**
- **1/2 cup (100g) sugar**
- **4 large egg yolks**
- **1/4 cup (30g) cornstarch**
- **2 tablespoons butter**
- **1 teaspoon vanilla extract**

For the Chocolate Glaze:

- **1/2 cup (120ml) heavy cream**
- **1 cup (175g) semi-sweet chocolate chips**

Instructions

1. Make the Choux Pastry:

1. **Preheat Oven**: Preheat your oven to 400°F (200°C). Line a baking sheet with parchment paper or a silicone baking mat.
2. **Combine Ingredients**: In a medium saucepan, combine the butter, water, and salt. Heat over medium heat until the butter is melted and the mixture starts to boil.
3. **Add Flour**: Remove from heat and add the flour all at once. Stir vigorously with a wooden spoon until the mixture pulls away from the sides of the pan and forms a smooth ball.
4. **Cook Dough**: Return the pan to medium heat and cook, stirring constantly, for about 1-2 minutes to dry out the dough slightly.
5. **Incorporate Eggs**: Transfer the dough to a mixing bowl and let it cool for a few minutes. Beat in the eggs one at a time, making sure each egg is fully incorporated before adding the next. The dough should be smooth and glossy.
6. **Pipe the Dough**: Transfer the dough to a pastry bag fitted with a plain round or star tip. Pipe long, slender shapes (about 4-6 inches long) onto the prepared baking sheet, spacing them a couple of inches apart.

7. **Bake**: Bake for 20-25 minutes or until the éclairs are golden brown and puffed. Do not open the oven door while baking. Let them cool completely on a wire rack.

2. Prepare the Pastry Cream:

1. **Heat Milk**: In a medium saucepan, heat the milk until it's just about to boil. Remove from heat.
2. **Whisk Yolks and Sugar**: In a bowl, whisk together the egg yolks and sugar until thick and pale. Add the cornstarch and mix until smooth.
3. **Combine and Cook**: Gradually whisk the hot milk into the egg mixture. Return the mixture to the saucepan and cook over medium heat, whisking constantly, until thickened and starting to boil.
4. **Finish**: Remove from heat and whisk in the butter and vanilla extract. Transfer the pastry cream to a bowl, cover with plastic wrap (pressing it directly onto the surface to prevent a skin from forming), and let it cool to room temperature.

3. Prepare the Chocolate Glaze:

1. **Heat Cream**: In a small saucepan, heat the heavy cream over medium heat until it just begins to simmer.
2. **Add Chocolate**: Remove from heat and add the chocolate chips. Let sit for a minute, then stir until the chocolate is completely melted and the glaze is smooth.

4. Assemble the Éclairs:

1. **Fill the Éclairs**: Once the éclairs are completely cooled, cut them in half lengthwise or make a small slit in the side. Fill each éclair with the cooled pastry cream using a pastry bag fitted with a small round tip or a spoon.
2. **Glaze**: Dip the top of each filled éclair into the chocolate glaze or use a spoon to drizzle the glaze over the top.
3. **Set**: Allow the chocolate glaze to set before serving.

Enjoy your homemade éclairs! They're best enjoyed fresh but can be stored in the refrigerator for a day or two.

Lemon Bars

Ingredients

For the Crust:

- **1 3/4 cups (220g) all-purpose flour**
- **1/2 cup (100g) granulated sugar**
- **1/2 teaspoon salt**
- **1 cup (225g) unsalted butter**, cold and cut into small pieces

For the Lemon Filling:

- **1 1/4 cups (250g) granulated sugar**
- **1/4 cup (30g) all-purpose flour**
- **4 large eggs**
- **2/3 cup (160ml) fresh lemon juice** (about 3-4 lemons)
- **1 tablespoon lemon zest** (from 1 lemon)
- **1/4 teaspoon salt**

For Dusting (Optional):

- **Powdered sugar**

Instructions

1. Make the Crust:

1. **Preheat Oven**: Preheat your oven to 350°F (175°C). Grease a 9x13-inch baking dish or line it with parchment paper, leaving some overhang for easy removal.
2. **Prepare Crust Mixture**: In a medium bowl, combine the flour, sugar, and salt. Add the cold butter pieces.
3. **Mix**: Use a pastry cutter, fork, or your fingers to mix the butter into the flour mixture until it resembles coarse crumbs.
4. **Press**: Press the mixture evenly into the bottom of the prepared baking dish.
5. **Bake**: Bake for 18-20 minutes, or until the edges are lightly golden. Remove from the oven and set aside.

2. Make the Lemon Filling:

1. **Combine Ingredients**: In a medium bowl, whisk together the sugar and flour.
2. **Add Eggs**: Add the eggs, one at a time, whisking well after each addition.
3. **Add Lemon Juice and Zest**: Stir in the lemon juice, lemon zest, and salt until well combined.
4. **Pour Over Crust**: Pour the lemon filling over the baked crust.

3. Bake:

1. **Bake Filling**: Return the dish to the oven and bake for an additional 20-25 minutes, or until the filling is set and the top is lightly golden.
2. **Cool**: Allow the lemon bars to cool completely in the pan on a wire rack. Once cooled, use the parchment overhang to lift the bars out of the pan and cut them into squares.

4. Dust and Serve:

1. **Dust with Powdered Sugar**: If desired, dust the cooled lemon bars with powdered sugar before serving.

Enjoy your homemade lemon bars! They're a bright and zesty treat that's perfect for any occasion.

Chocolate Chip Cookies

Ingredients

- 1 cup (225g) unsalted butter, at room temperature
- 1 cup (200g) granulated sugar
- 1 cup (220g) packed brown sugar
- 2 large eggs
- 1 teaspoon vanilla extract
- 3 cups (375g) all-purpose flour
- 1 teaspoon baking soda
- 1/2 teaspoon baking powder
- 1/2 teaspoon salt
- 2 cups (340g) semisweet chocolate chips

Instructions

1. Preheat Oven:

1. **Preheat Oven**: Preheat your oven to 350°F (175°C). Line baking sheets with parchment paper or silicone baking mats.

2. Prepare the Dough:

1. **Cream Butter and Sugars**: In a large bowl, beat the butter, granulated sugar, and brown sugar together until light and fluffy.
2. **Add Eggs and Vanilla**: Beat in the eggs one at a time, followed by the vanilla extract.
3. **Combine Dry Ingredients**: In a separate bowl, whisk together the flour, baking soda, baking powder, and salt.
4. **Mix Dry and Wet Ingredients**: Gradually add the dry ingredients to the wet ingredients, mixing just until combined. Avoid overmixing.
5. **Stir in Chocolate Chips**: Fold in the chocolate chips until evenly distributed.

3. Bake the Cookies:

1. **Scoop Dough**: Use a cookie scoop or spoon to drop rounded tablespoons of dough onto the prepared baking sheets, spacing them about 2 inches apart.
2. **Bake**: Bake for 10-12 minutes, or until the edges are golden brown but the centers are still soft. The cookies will continue to set as they cool.
3. **Cool**: Let the cookies cool on the baking sheets for a few minutes before transferring them to wire racks to cool completely.

4. Enjoy:

1. **Serve**: Enjoy your homemade chocolate chip cookies with a glass of milk or on their own!

Tips for Perfect Cookies

- **Butter Temperature**: Make sure your butter is at room temperature for the best texture.
- **Chill Dough**: If you prefer thicker cookies, chill the dough for about 30 minutes before baking.
- **Mix-Ins**: Feel free to add nuts, dried fruit, or other mix-ins to customize your cookies.

Enjoy baking and indulging in these classic chocolate chip cookies!

Coconut Cream Pie

Ingredients

For the Pie Crust:

- 1 1/2 cups (190g) all-purpose flour
- 1/2 cup (100g) granulated sugar
- 1/2 teaspoon salt
- 1/2 cup (115g) unsalted butter, cold and cut into small pieces
- 1/4 cup (60ml) ice water (more if needed)

For the Coconut Cream Filling:

- 1/2 cup (100g) granulated sugar
- 1/4 cup (30g) cornstarch
- 1/4 teaspoon salt
- 2 3/4 cups (660ml) whole milk
- 4 large egg yolks
- 2 tablespoons unsalted butter
- 1 cup (80g) shredded sweetened coconut (toasted if desired)
- 1 teaspoon vanilla extract
- 1 teaspoon coconut extract (optional, for extra coconut flavor)

For the Topping:

- 1 cup (240ml) heavy cream
- 2 tablespoons powdered sugar
- 1/2 teaspoon vanilla extract
- 1/2 cup (40g) toasted shredded coconut (for garnish)

Instructions

1. Prepare the Pie Crust:

1. **Preheat Oven**: Preheat your oven to 375°F (190°C).
2. **Make Dough**: In a food processor, combine the flour, sugar, and salt. Add the cold butter and pulse until the mixture resembles coarse crumbs. Gradually add the ice water, a tablespoon at a time, until the dough comes together.
3. **Roll Out Dough**: Turn the dough out onto a lightly floured surface and roll it out to fit a 9-inch pie dish. Transfer the dough to the dish and press it into the bottom and sides.
4. **Chill**: Refrigerate the pie crust for about 15 minutes to prevent it from shrinking.
5. **Bake**: Line the crust with parchment paper and fill with pie weights or dried beans. Bake for 15 minutes, then remove the weights and parchment paper, and bake for an additional 5-7 minutes until the crust is golden brown. Let it cool completely.

2. Make the Coconut Cream Filling:

1. **Combine Dry Ingredients**: In a medium saucepan, whisk together the sugar, cornstarch, and salt.
2. **Add Milk**: Gradually whisk in the milk. Cook over medium heat, stirring constantly until the mixture begins to thicken and comes to a gentle boil.
3. **Temper Egg Yolks**: In a small bowl, lightly beat the egg yolks. Gradually whisk in about 1/2 cup of the hot milk mixture to temper the yolks. Then whisk the tempered yolks back into the saucepan.
4. **Cook Filling**: Continue to cook the mixture for another 2-3 minutes until it thickens further. Remove from heat and stir in the butter, shredded coconut, vanilla extract, and coconut extract (if using).
5. **Cool**: Pour the filling into the cooled pie crust, smoothing the top with a spatula. Cover with plastic wrap, pressing it directly onto the surface of the filling to prevent a skin from forming. Refrigerate for at least 4 hours or until set.

3. Prepare the Topping:

1. **Whip Cream**: In a medium bowl, beat the heavy cream with an electric mixer until soft peaks form. Add the powdered sugar and vanilla extract, and continue to beat until stiff peaks form.
2. **Top Pie**: Spread or pipe the whipped cream over the chilled coconut cream filling. Garnish with toasted shredded coconut.

4. Serve:

1. **Slice and Enjoy**: Slice the pie and serve chilled. Enjoy your homemade Coconut Cream Pie!

Tips:

- **Toasted Coconut**: Toast shredded coconut in a dry skillet over medium heat until golden brown, stirring frequently. This adds extra flavor and a nice crunch.
- **Chilling**: Make sure the pie is well-chilled before serving to ensure the filling is firm and easy to slice.

Enjoy your Coconut Cream Pie! It's a delightful treat that's perfect for special occasions or just a sweet indulgence.

Pumpkin Pie

Ingredients

For the Pie Crust:

- **1 1/2 cups (190g) all-purpose flour**
- **1/2 cup (100g) granulated sugar**
- **1/2 teaspoon salt**
- **1/2 cup (115g) unsalted butter**, cold and cut into small pieces
- **1/4 cup (60ml) ice water** (more if needed)

For the Pumpkin Filling:

- **1 can (15 oz or 425g) pumpkin puree** (not pumpkin pie filling)
- **3/4 cup (150g) granulated sugar**
- **1/2 teaspoon salt**
- **1 teaspoon ground cinnamon**
- **1/2 teaspoon ground ginger**
- **1/4 teaspoon ground cloves**
- **1/4 teaspoon ground nutmeg**
- **2 large eggs**
- **1 cup (240ml) heavy cream**
- **1/2 cup (120ml) whole milk**

For the Whipped Cream (Optional):

- **1 cup (240ml) heavy cream**
- **2 tablespoons powdered sugar**
- **1 teaspoon vanilla extract**

Instructions

1. Prepare the Pie Crust:

1. **Preheat Oven**: Preheat your oven to 375°F (190°C).
2. **Make Dough**: In a food processor, combine the flour, sugar, and salt. Add the cold butter and pulse until the mixture resembles coarse crumbs. Gradually add the ice water, a tablespoon at a time, until the dough comes together.
3. **Roll Out Dough**: Turn the dough out onto a lightly floured surface and roll it out to fit a 9-inch pie dish. Transfer the dough to the dish and press it into the bottom and sides.
4. **Chill**: Refrigerate the pie crust for about 15 minutes to prevent it from shrinking.
5. **Pre-Bake**: Line the crust with parchment paper and fill with pie weights or dried beans. Bake for 15 minutes, then remove the weights and parchment paper, and bake for an additional 5-7 minutes until the crust is lightly golden. Let it cool slightly.

2. Make the Pumpkin Filling:

1. **Combine Ingredients**: In a large bowl, whisk together the pumpkin puree, sugar, salt, cinnamon, ginger, cloves, and nutmeg.
2. **Add Eggs and Dairy**: Whisk in the eggs until well combined. Then stir in the heavy cream and milk until the mixture is smooth.
3. **Pour Filling**: Pour the pumpkin filling into the pre-baked pie crust.

3. Bake the Pie:

1. **Bake**: Bake the pie at 375°F (190°C) for 50-60 minutes, or until the filling is set and the crust is golden brown. The center of the pie should be slightly jiggly but will firm up as it cools.
2. **Cool**: Allow the pie to cool completely on a wire rack before serving. This can take a few hours.

4. Prepare the Whipped Cream (Optional):

1. **Whip Cream**: In a medium bowl, beat the heavy cream with an electric mixer until soft peaks form. Add the powdered sugar and vanilla extract, and continue to beat until stiff peaks form.
2. **Serve**: Spread or pipe the whipped cream over the cooled pie before serving.

Tips:

- **Pumpkin Purée**: Use pure pumpkin purée, not pumpkin pie filling, which is pre-sweetened and spiced.
- **Spice Adjustment**: Adjust the spices to your taste; some people like more cinnamon or nutmeg.
- **Crust Lattice**: For a decorative touch, you can make a lattice crust or add pie crust cutouts.

Enjoy your homemade Pumpkin Pie! It's a comforting, classic dessert that's sure to be a hit at any gathering.

Churros

Ingredients

For the Churros:

- 1 cup (240ml) water
- 1/2 cup (115g) unsalted butter
- 2 tablespoons granulated sugar
- 1/4 teaspoon salt
- 1 cup (125g) all-purpose flour
- 3 large eggs

For the Cinnamon Sugar Coating:

- 1/2 cup (100g) granulated sugar
- 1 tablespoon ground cinnamon

For Frying:

- **Vegetable oil** (for frying, about 2-3 cups)

For the Chocolate Dipping Sauce (Optional):

- 1/2 cup (120ml) heavy cream
- 1 cup (175g) semi-sweet chocolate chips
- 1 tablespoon light corn syrup (optional, for a shinier sauce)

Instructions

1. Prepare the Churros Dough:

1. **Combine Ingredients**: In a medium saucepan, combine the water, butter, sugar, and salt. Heat over medium heat until the butter is melted and the mixture starts to boil.
2. **Add Flour**: Remove from heat and add the flour all at once. Stir vigorously with a wooden spoon until the mixture forms a smooth ball and pulls away from the sides of the pan.
3. **Cool Dough**: Let the dough cool for about 5 minutes. Then beat in the eggs one at a time, making sure each egg is fully incorporated before adding the next. The dough should be smooth and slightly sticky.
4. **Transfer Dough**: Transfer the dough to a pastry bag fitted with a large star tip.

2. Prepare the Cinnamon Sugar Coating:

1. **Mix**: In a shallow bowl, combine the granulated sugar and cinnamon.

3. Fry the Churros:

1. **Heat Oil**: In a deep saucepan or large pot, heat the vegetable oil to 350°F (175°C). Use a candy or deep-frying thermometer to check the temperature.
2. **Pipe and Fry**: Pipe 4-6 inch strips of dough into the hot oil, using scissors or a knife to cut the dough from the pastry bag. Fry a few churros at a time, being careful not to overcrowd the pot.
3. **Cook**: Fry the churros for about 2-3 minutes per side, or until they are golden brown and crispy.
4. **Drain**: Use a slotted spoon to remove the churros from the oil and drain them on a paper towel-lined plate.

4. Coat with Cinnamon Sugar:

1. **Coat**: While the churros are still warm, roll them in the cinnamon sugar mixture until fully coated.

5. Prepare the Chocolate Dipping Sauce (Optional):

1. **Heat Cream**: In a small saucepan, heat the heavy cream until it just starts to simmer.
2. **Add Chocolate**: Remove from heat and add the chocolate chips and corn syrup (if using). Let it sit for a minute, then stir until smooth and fully combined.

6. Serve:

1. **Enjoy**: Serve the churros warm, with the chocolate dipping sauce on the side if desired.

Tips:

- **Oil Temperature**: Maintain the oil temperature around 350°F (175°C) to ensure the churros cook evenly and don't become too greasy.
- **Piping Tip**: A large star tip gives churros their classic ridged shape, but you can use a plain tip if you prefer.

Enjoy making and eating your homemade churros! They're perfect for a special treat or for sharing with friends and family.

Baklava

Ingredients

For the Baklava:

- **1 package (16 oz or 450g) phyllo dough**, thawed (usually comes in 1 lb packages)
- **2 cups (225g) finely chopped nuts** (a mix of walnuts, pistachios, and almonds works well)
- **1 teaspoon ground cinnamon**
- **1 cup (225g) unsalted butter**, melted

For the Honey Syrup:

- **1 cup (240ml) water**
- **1 cup (225g) granulated sugar**
- **1/2 cup (120ml) honey**
- **1/2 teaspoon vanilla extract**
- **1/2 teaspoon lemon juice**

Instructions

1. Prepare the Nut Filling:

1. **Combine Ingredients**: In a bowl, mix the finely chopped nuts with the ground cinnamon. Set aside.

2. Prepare the Phyllo Dough:

1. **Preheat Oven**: Preheat your oven to 350°F (175°C). Grease a 9x13-inch baking dish or a similar-sized dish with melted butter.
2. **Assemble Layers**: Unroll the phyllo dough and cover it with a damp towel to prevent it from drying out. Place one sheet of phyllo dough into the greased baking dish and brush it with melted butter. Repeat this process, layering and buttering each sheet until you have about 8-10 layers.
3. **Add Nut Filling**: Evenly sprinkle a portion of the nut mixture over the layered phyllo.
4. **Layer and Repeat**: Continue layering with another 6-8 sheets of phyllo, each brushed with melted butter, then add another layer of nuts. Repeat until all the nuts are used, finishing with a final 6-8 layers of phyllo, each brushed with butter.

3. Cut and Bake:

1. **Cut the Baklava**: Using a sharp knife, cut the baklava into diamond or square shapes, cutting all the way through to the bottom. This helps the syrup soak in evenly.
2. **Bake**: Bake in the preheated oven for 45-50 minutes, or until the baklava is golden brown and crisp.

4. Prepare the Honey Syrup:

1. **Combine Ingredients**: While the baklava is baking, in a saucepan, combine the water, sugar, honey, vanilla extract, and lemon juice. Bring to a boil over medium heat, stirring occasionally.
2. **Simmer**: Reduce heat and let the syrup simmer for about 10 minutes, or until it slightly thickens. Remove from heat and let it cool.

5. Finish the Baklava:

1. **Add Syrup**: As soon as the baklava comes out of the oven, pour the cooled honey syrup evenly over the hot baklava. Allow the baklava to cool completely in the pan; this will help the syrup soak in and the layers to set.

Tips:

- **Phyllo Dough Handling**: Keep the phyllo dough covered with a damp towel to prevent it from drying out while you work with it.
- **Butter Application**: Be generous with buttering each layer of phyllo to ensure a crispy texture.
- **Nuts**: Feel free to use your favorite nuts or a combination, and make sure they are finely chopped for even distribution and flavor.

Enjoy your homemade baklava! It's a delicious treat with a wonderful balance of sweet and nutty flavors, perfect for special occasions or as a luxurious dessert.

Pecan Pie

Ingredients

For the Pie Crust:

- 1 1/2 cups (190g) all-purpose flour
- 1/2 cup (100g) granulated sugar
- 1/2 teaspoon salt
- 1/2 cup (115g) unsalted butter, cold and cut into small pieces
- 1/4 cup (60ml) ice water (more if needed)

For the Pecan Filling:

- 1 cup (200g) granulated sugar
- 1/2 cup (100g) packed brown sugar
- 1/4 teaspoon salt
- 1/2 cup (115g) unsalted butter, melted
- 4 large eggs
- 1 cup (240ml) light corn syrup (or dark corn syrup for a deeper flavor)
- 1 teaspoon vanilla extract
- 2 cups (200g) pecan halves

Instructions

1. Prepare the Pie Crust:

1. **Preheat Oven**: Preheat your oven to 375°F (190°C).
2. **Make Dough**: In a food processor, combine the flour, sugar, and salt. Add the cold butter and pulse until the mixture resembles coarse crumbs. Gradually add the ice water, a tablespoon at a time, until the dough comes together.
3. **Roll Out Dough**: Turn the dough out onto a lightly floured surface and roll it out to fit a 9-inch pie dish. Transfer the dough to the dish and press it into the bottom and sides.
4. **Chill**: Refrigerate the pie crust for about 15 minutes to prevent it from shrinking.
5. **Pre-Bake**: Line the crust with parchment paper and fill with pie weights or dried beans. Bake for 10 minutes, then remove the weights and parchment paper, and bake for an additional 5 minutes. Let it cool slightly.

2. Prepare the Pecan Filling:

1. **Mix Ingredients**: In a large bowl, whisk together the granulated sugar, brown sugar, and salt. Add the melted butter and mix until combined.
2. **Add Eggs and Syrup**: Whisk in the eggs one at a time, then stir in the corn syrup and vanilla extract until smooth.
3. **Add Pecans**: Fold in the pecan halves.

3. Assemble and Bake:

1. **Pour Filling**: Pour the pecan filling into the pre-baked pie crust, spreading the pecans evenly.
2. **Bake**: Bake in the preheated oven for 50-60 minutes, or until the filling is set and slightly puffed. The center should be firm but slightly jiggly.
3. **Cool**: Allow the pie to cool completely on a wire rack before slicing. This allows the filling to set properly.

Tips:

- **Corn Syrup**: Light corn syrup is commonly used for a lighter flavor, but dark corn syrup will give a richer, more caramel-like taste.
- **Prevent Over-Browning**: If the edges of the crust start to brown too quickly, cover them with aluminum foil to prevent burning.
- **Cooling**: Make sure to let the pie cool completely before slicing. This ensures that the filling will set properly and slice cleanly.

Enjoy your homemade Pecan Pie! It's a sweet and satisfying treat that's sure to be a hit at any gathering.

White Chocolate Raspberry Cheesecake

Ingredients

For the Crust:

- **1 1/2 cups (150g) graham cracker crumbs** (about 12 graham crackers, crushed)
- **1/4 cup (50g) granulated sugar**
- **1/2 cup (115g) unsalted butter**, melted

For the Cheesecake Filling:

- **12 oz (340g) cream cheese**, at room temperature
- **1 cup (200g) granulated sugar**
- **1/2 cup (120ml) sour cream**
- **1/2 cup (120ml) heavy cream**
- **1 teaspoon vanilla extract**
- **3 large eggs**, at room temperature
- **6 oz (170g) white chocolate**, chopped
- **1 cup (240ml) raspberry puree** (about 2 cups fresh or frozen raspberries blended and strained to remove seeds)

For the Raspberry Swirl:

- **1/2 cup (120ml) raspberry puree** (from the 1 cup used above)
- **1/4 cup (50g) granulated sugar**

Instructions

1. Prepare the Crust:

1. **Preheat Oven**: Preheat your oven to 325°F (160°C).
2. **Combine Crust Ingredients**: In a medium bowl, mix the graham cracker crumbs, sugar, and melted butter until well combined.
3. **Press Crust**: Press the mixture into the bottom of a 9-inch springform pan to form an even layer. Use the back of a spoon or a flat-bottomed glass to press it firmly.
4. **Bake**: Bake the crust for 10 minutes, then remove from the oven and let it cool.

2. Prepare the Cheesecake Filling:

1. **Melt White Chocolate**: In a heatproof bowl over simmering water (double boiler) or in the microwave, melt the white chocolate. Stir until smooth and let it cool slightly.
2. **Beat Cream Cheese**: In a large mixing bowl, beat the cream cheese until smooth and creamy.
3. **Add Sugar**: Gradually add the granulated sugar and beat until well combined.

4. **Add Sour Cream and Heavy Cream**: Mix in the sour cream, heavy cream, and vanilla extract.
5. **Add Eggs**: Add the eggs one at a time, mixing on low speed until just combined after each addition. Be careful not to overmix.
6. **Add White Chocolate**: Fold in the melted white chocolate until evenly distributed.
7. **Add Raspberry Puree**: Gently fold in 1 cup of raspberry puree.

3. Prepare the Raspberry Swirl:

1. **Combine Ingredients**: In a small saucepan, combine the 1/2 cup raspberry puree and granulated sugar. Heat over medium heat until the sugar is dissolved and the puree slightly thickens. Let it cool.

4. Assemble and Bake:

1. **Prepare Pan**: Wrap the bottom of the springform pan with aluminum foil to prevent leaks. Place the pan in a larger roasting pan.
2. **Pour Filling**: Pour the cheesecake filling into the prepared crust. Smooth the top with a spatula.
3. **Add Raspberry Swirl**: Drop spoonfuls of the raspberry swirl mixture onto the top of the cheesecake. Use a toothpick or knife to gently swirl the raspberry mixture into the cheesecake.
4. **Bake**: Pour hot water into the roasting pan to create a water bath for the cheesecake. Bake in the preheated oven for 60-70 minutes, or until the cheesecake is set around the edges but still slightly jiggly in the center.
5. **Turn Off Oven**: Turn off the oven and crack the door slightly. Let the cheesecake cool in the oven for 1 hour to prevent cracking.
6. **Chill**: Remove the cheesecake from the oven and water bath. Refrigerate for at least 4 hours or overnight to fully set.

Tips:

- **Water Bath**: The water bath helps to evenly cook the cheesecake and prevent cracks. Ensure the foil is tightly wrapped around the pan to prevent water from leaking in.
- **Raspberry Puree**: For a smoother cheesecake, strain the raspberry puree to remove seeds before adding it to the batter.
- **Room Temperature Ingredients**: Make sure all your ingredients, especially cream cheese and eggs, are at room temperature for a smooth filling.

Enjoy your White Chocolate Raspberry Cheesecake! It's a luxurious dessert with a perfect balance of creamy, sweet, and tart flavors.

Mocha Mousse

Ingredients

- **4 oz (115g) semisweet or bittersweet chocolate**, chopped
- **2 tablespoons brewed espresso** (or strong coffee)
- **1/2 cup (120ml) heavy cream**, plus more for whipped cream (optional)
- **2 large eggs**, separated
- **1/4 cup (50g) granulated sugar**
- **1/4 teaspoon cream of tartar** (optional, helps stabilize the egg whites)
- **1 teaspoon vanilla extract**

For Garnish (Optional):

- **Whipped cream**
- **Chocolate shavings or curls**
- **Coffee beans**

Instructions

1. Melt Chocolate:

1. **Melt Chocolate**: In a heatproof bowl over simmering water (double boiler) or in the microwave, melt the chocolate with the brewed espresso. Stir until smooth. Let it cool slightly.

2. Prepare the Mousse Base:

1. **Beat Egg Yolks**: In a medium bowl, whisk the egg yolks. Gradually add half of the granulated sugar, continuing to whisk until the mixture is pale and slightly thickened. Fold in the melted chocolate mixture.
2. **Whip Cream**: In a separate bowl, whip the 1/2 cup heavy cream until soft peaks form. Gently fold the whipped cream into the chocolate mixture.

3. Prepare the Meringue:

1. **Beat Egg Whites**: In a clean, dry bowl, beat the egg whites with a hand mixer or stand mixer until they start to froth. Add the cream of tartar (if using) and continue to beat until soft peaks form.
2. **Add Sugar**: Gradually add the remaining granulated sugar, beating until the egg whites are glossy and stiff peaks form.

4. Combine and Chill:

1. **Fold Meringue**: Gently fold the meringue into the chocolate mixture in thirds, being careful not to deflate the mixture. The mousse should be light and airy.

2. **Chill**: Spoon the mousse into individual serving dishes or glasses. Refrigerate for at least 2 hours, or until set.

5. Garnish and Serve:

1. **Top with Whipped Cream**: If desired, top each serving with a dollop of whipped cream.
2. **Garnish**: Garnish with chocolate shavings or curls, and a few coffee beans if you like.

Tips:

- **Egg Whites**: Make sure the bowl and beaters are completely clean and free of grease for the egg whites to whip properly.
- **Chocolate**: Use good-quality chocolate for the best flavor.
- **Coffee**: For a more intense coffee flavor, you can use strong coffee or espresso. Adjust the amount based on your taste preference.

Enjoy your Mocha Mousse! It's a perfect dessert for coffee and chocolate lovers, with a wonderfully rich and creamy texture.

Peanut Butter Pie

Ingredients

For the Crust:

- **1 1/2 cups (150g) graham cracker crumbs** (about 12 graham crackers, crushed)
- **1/4 cup (50g) granulated sugar**
- **1/2 cup (115g) unsalted butter**, melted

For the Filling:

- **1 cup (240ml) heavy cream**
- **1 cup (250g) creamy peanut butter**
- **8 oz (225g) cream cheese**, softened
- **1 cup (100g) powdered sugar**
- **1 teaspoon vanilla extract**

For the Topping:

- **1 cup (240ml) heavy cream**
- **2 tablespoons powdered sugar**
- **1/2 teaspoon vanilla extract**
- **Chopped peanuts** (for garnish)
- **Chocolate shavings or chocolate sauce** (optional, for garnish)

Instructions

1. Prepare the Crust:

1. **Preheat Oven**: Preheat your oven to 350°F (175°C).
2. **Combine Crust Ingredients**: In a medium bowl, mix the graham cracker crumbs, sugar, and melted butter until well combined.
3. **Press Crust**: Press the mixture into the bottom and up the sides of a 9-inch pie dish, using the back of a spoon or the bottom of a glass to pack it down firmly.
4. **Bake**: Bake the crust for 8-10 minutes, or until it is lightly golden. Let it cool completely before adding the filling.

2. Prepare the Filling:

1. **Whip Cream**: In a mixing bowl, whip the heavy cream until soft peaks form. Set aside.
2. **Mix Peanut Butter Filling**: In another large bowl, beat the peanut butter and cream cheese until smooth. Gradually add the powdered sugar and vanilla extract, mixing until well combined.
3. **Fold in Whipped Cream**: Gently fold the whipped cream into the peanut butter mixture until fully combined and smooth.

3. Assemble the Pie:

1. **Fill Crust**: Spoon the peanut butter filling into the cooled pie crust and smooth the top with a spatula.
2. **Chill**: Refrigerate the pie for at least 4 hours, or until the filling is set.

4. Prepare the Topping:

1. **Whip Cream**: In a mixing bowl, beat the heavy cream, powdered sugar, and vanilla extract until stiff peaks form.
2. **Top Pie**: Spread or pipe the whipped cream over the chilled pie.
3. **Garnish**: Sprinkle with chopped peanuts and add chocolate shavings or drizzle with chocolate sauce if desired.

Tips:

- **Cream Cheese**: Make sure the cream cheese is softened to room temperature to avoid lumps in the filling.
- **Peanut Butter**: Use creamy peanut butter for a smooth filling. If you prefer a chunkier texture, you can use crunchy peanut butter.
- **Chilling**: Allow the pie to chill for a sufficient amount of time to ensure that it sets properly and the flavors meld together.

Enjoy your homemade Peanut Butter Pie! It's a rich, creamy dessert that's sure to be a hit with peanut butter lovers.

Brown Butter Blondies

Ingredients

For the Blondies:

- 1 cup (226g) unsalted butter
- 1 1/2 cups (300g) brown sugar, packed
- 2 large eggs
- 2 teaspoons vanilla extract
- 2 1/4 cups (280g) all-purpose flour
- 1/2 teaspoon baking powder
- 1/2 teaspoon baking soda
- 1/2 teaspoon salt
- 1 cup (175g) chocolate chips (or chunks)

Optional Add-Ins:

- 1 cup (100g) chopped nuts (e.g., pecans, walnuts, or cashews)
- 1/2 cup (90g) toffee bits

Instructions

1. Brown the Butter:

1. **Melt Butter**: In a medium saucepan over medium heat, melt the butter.
2. **Brown Butter**: Continue cooking the butter, swirling the pan occasionally, until it turns golden brown and has a nutty aroma. Be careful not to burn it. Remove from heat and let it cool slightly.

2. Prepare the Blondie Batter:

1. **Preheat Oven**: Preheat your oven to 350°F (175°C). Grease and line an 8x8-inch (20x20 cm) baking pan with parchment paper, leaving an overhang for easy removal.
2. **Mix Sugar and Butter**: In a large bowl, combine the brown sugar and brown butter, mixing until smooth.
3. **Add Eggs and Vanilla**: Beat in the eggs one at a time, followed by the vanilla extract, until well combined.
4. **Combine Dry Ingredients**: In a separate bowl, whisk together the flour, baking powder, baking soda, and salt.
5. **Combine Wet and Dry Ingredients**: Gradually add the dry ingredients to the wet ingredients, mixing until just combined. Fold in the chocolate chips (and optional add-ins if using).

3. Bake:

1. **Transfer Batter**: Spread the batter evenly in the prepared baking pan.
2. **Bake**: Bake for 25-30 minutes, or until a toothpick inserted into the center comes out with a few moist crumbs. The edges should be golden brown, and the center should be set but still soft.

4. Cool and Serve:

1. **Cool**: Allow the blondies to cool completely in the pan on a wire rack before cutting into squares.
2. **Serve**: Enjoy them as a sweet treat with a glass of milk or a cup of coffee!

Tips:

- **Butter Temperature**: Let the brown butter cool slightly before mixing it with the sugar to avoid cooking the eggs when combined.
- **Mix-Ins**: Feel free to customize with your favorite mix-ins like dried fruit, or different types of chocolate.
- **Storage**: Store the blondies in an airtight container at room temperature for up to a week, or refrigerate for longer storage.

Enjoy your homemade Brown Butter Blondies! They have a rich, toasty flavor with a perfect balance of sweetness and texture.

Cherry Clafoutis

Ingredients

- **1 pound (450g) fresh cherries** (pitted if preferred)
- **3 large eggs**
- **1 cup (240ml) whole milk**
- **1/2 cup (100g) granulated sugar**
- **1/2 cup (65g) all-purpose flour**
- **1/4 teaspoon salt**
- **1 teaspoon vanilla extract**
- **1 tablespoon unsalted butter** (for greasing the pan)
- **Powdered sugar** (for dusting, optional)

Instructions

1. Prepare the Cherries:

1. **Preheat Oven**: Preheat your oven to 375°F (190°C).
2. **Prep Cherries**: Wash and pit the cherries. You can leave the pits in for a more traditional clafoutis, or pit them for convenience.

2. Prepare the Batter:

1. **Blend Batter**: In a blender or food processor, combine the eggs, milk, granulated sugar, flour, salt, and vanilla extract. Blend until smooth and frothy.

3. Prepare the Pan:

1. **Grease Pan**: Grease a 9-inch (23 cm) pie dish or a similar-sized baking dish with the butter.

4. Assemble and Bake:

1. **Arrange Cherries**: Scatter the cherries evenly in the bottom of the greased dish.
2. **Pour Batter**: Pour the batter evenly over the cherries.
3. **Bake**: Bake in the preheated oven for 35-45 minutes, or until the clafoutis is puffed and golden brown and a knife inserted into the center comes out clean. The clafoutis should be set but still slightly jiggly in the middle.

5. Cool and Serve:

1. **Cool**: Allow the clafoutis to cool slightly before serving. It can be enjoyed warm, at room temperature, or even cold.
2. **Dust with Powdered Sugar**: If desired, dust with powdered sugar before serving.

Tips:

- **Cherries**: Fresh cherries work best, but you can use frozen cherries if fresh ones are not available. Just make sure to thaw and drain them well.
- **Batter Consistency**: The batter should be somewhat thin; it's similar to a pancake or crepe batter.
- **Serving**: Clafoutis can be served as a dessert or even as a sweet breakfast treat.

Enjoy your Cherry Clafoutis! It's a delightful and rustic dessert that's perfect for showcasing fresh cherries in a simple yet delicious way.

Mango Sorbet

Ingredients

- **4 cups (about 4 large) ripe mangoes**, peeled, pitted, and cubed (you can also use frozen mango chunks)
- **1/2 cup (100g) granulated sugar** (adjust to taste)
- **1/2 cup (120ml) fresh lime juice** (about 2-3 limes)
- **1/2 cup (120ml) water**
- **1 tablespoon light corn syrup** (optional, helps with texture)

Instructions

1. Prepare Mango Puree:

1. **Blend Mangoes**: In a blender or food processor, blend the mango cubes until smooth. You should have about 3 cups of mango puree.

2. Make the Sorbet Base:

1. **Combine Ingredients**: In a mixing bowl, combine the mango puree, granulated sugar, fresh lime juice, and water. Stir until the sugar is completely dissolved. If using corn syrup, add it here and mix well.

3. Chill the Mixture:

1. **Refrigerate**: Cover and refrigerate the mixture for at least 1 hour, or until well chilled. This step ensures a smoother texture in the final sorbet.

4. Freeze the Sorbet:

1. **Using an Ice Cream Maker**: Pour the chilled mixture into an ice cream maker and churn according to the manufacturer's instructions, usually about 20-25 minutes, until it reaches a soft-serve consistency.
2. **Without an Ice Cream Maker**: If you don't have an ice cream maker, pour the mixture into a shallow dish and place it in the freezer. Stir vigorously with a fork every 30 minutes to break up ice crystals, until the sorbet is frozen and fluffy (about 3-4 hours).

5. Serve:

1. **Scoop**: Once the sorbet is fully frozen, scoop it into bowls or glasses. Let it sit at room temperature for a few minutes to soften slightly before serving if needed.

Tips:

- **Mango Ripeness**: Use ripe mangoes for the best flavor. They should be sweet and slightly soft to the touch.
- **Sugar Adjustment**: Adjust the sugar according to the sweetness of your mangoes and your taste preference.
- **Texture**: The corn syrup helps create a smoother texture, but you can omit it if you prefer.

Enjoy your homemade Mango Sorbet! It's a delightful, fruity treat that's sure to cool you down and satisfy your sweet tooth.

Chocolate Truffles

Ingredients

For the Truffle Filling:

- **8 oz (225g) semisweet or bittersweet chocolate**, chopped
- **1 cup (240ml) heavy cream**
- **2 tablespoons unsalted butter**, at room temperature
- **1 teaspoon vanilla extract** (or other flavorings like liqueur, coffee, or extracts)

For the Coatings (optional):

- **Cocoa powder**
- **Powdered sugar**
- **Chopped nuts** (e.g., almonds, hazelnuts, or pecans)
- **Shredded coconut**
- **Chocolate sprinkles**
- **Crushed cookies** (e.g., graham crackers or Oreos)

Instructions

1. Make the Truffle Filling:

1. **Heat Cream**: In a small saucepan over medium heat, bring the heavy cream just to a simmer. Remove from heat before it starts boiling.
2. **Add Chocolate**: Place the chopped chocolate in a heatproof bowl. Pour the hot cream over the chocolate and let it sit for about 5 minutes to melt the chocolate.
3. **Stir**: Gently stir the mixture until smooth. Add the butter and vanilla extract (or any additional flavorings) and stir until fully combined and smooth.

2. Chill the Ganache:

1. **Cool**: Let the ganache cool to room temperature, then cover and refrigerate for at least 2 hours, or until it is firm enough to handle.

3. Shape the Truffles:

1. **Scoop**: Using a small cookie scoop or a spoon, scoop out small portions of the ganache and roll them between your hands to form smooth balls. If the ganache becomes too soft, refrigerate it briefly to firm up.
2. **Coat**: Roll each truffle in your choice of coating. You can use cocoa powder for a classic look, or get creative with nuts, coconut, or crushed cookies.

4. Chill and Serve:

1. **Chill Again**: Place the coated truffles on a baking sheet lined with parchment paper and refrigerate them for another 30 minutes to set.
2. **Serve**: Serve the truffles chilled or at room temperature. Store them in an airtight container in the refrigerator for up to 2 weeks.

Tips:

- **Chocolate Quality**: Use high-quality chocolate for the best flavor and smooth texture.
- **Flavored Truffles**: Experiment with different extracts (like almond or peppermint) or add a splash of your favorite liqueur to the ganache for unique flavor variations.
- **Coating Ideas**: You can also dip the truffles in melted chocolate for a more decadent finish. Simply chill the truffles until firm, then dip them in melted chocolate and let them set.

Enjoy making and indulging in your homemade chocolate truffles! They're a perfect treat for special occasions or simply as a luxurious snack.

Pavlova

Ingredients

For the Meringue Base:

- **4 large egg whites**, at room temperature
- **1 cup (200g) granulated sugar**
- **1 teaspoon cornstarch**
- **1 teaspoon white vinegar** (or lemon juice)
- **1/2 teaspoon vanilla extract**

For the Topping:

- **1 cup (240ml) heavy cream**
- **2 tablespoons powdered sugar**
- **1 teaspoon vanilla extract**
- **Fresh fruit** (such as strawberries, kiwi, blueberries, or passion fruit)
- **Mint leaves** (for garnish, optional)

Instructions

1. Prepare the Meringue Base:

1. **Preheat Oven**: Preheat your oven to 250°F (120°C). Line a baking sheet with parchment paper.
2. **Beat Egg Whites**: In a clean, dry mixing bowl, beat the egg whites using an electric mixer or stand mixer on medium speed until soft peaks form.
3. **Add Sugar**: Gradually add the granulated sugar, a few tablespoons at a time, beating on high speed until the meringue is thick and glossy and forms stiff peaks.
4. **Add Cornstarch and Vinegar**: Gently fold in the cornstarch, vinegar, and vanilla extract until fully combined. The cornstarch helps stabilize the meringue and gives it a marshmallow-like center.

2. Shape and Bake:

1. **Shape Meringue**: Spoon or pipe the meringue onto the prepared baking sheet, shaping it into a round disc about 8-10 inches (20-25 cm) in diameter. Create a slight well in the center to hold the toppings.
2. **Bake**: Bake in the preheated oven for 1 hour to 1 hour 15 minutes, or until the meringue is dry and crisp on the outside and can be easily lifted off the parchment paper. It should be white or very light beige in color. Turn off the oven and let the meringue cool completely in the oven with the door slightly ajar.

3. Prepare the Topping:

1. **Whip Cream**: In a mixing bowl, beat the heavy cream with the powdered sugar and vanilla extract until soft peaks form.
2. **Prepare Fruit**: Wash and slice the fresh fruit as desired. If using passion fruit, scoop out the seeds and pulp.

4. Assemble and Serve:

1. **Top Meringue**: Carefully transfer the cooled meringue to a serving platter. Spread or pipe the whipped cream over the top of the meringue.
2. **Add Fruit**: Arrange the fresh fruit on top of the whipped cream.
3. **Garnish**: Optionally, garnish with mint leaves for a fresh touch.

Tips:

- **Egg Whites**: Ensure there is no yolk in the egg whites and that the bowl and beaters are completely clean and free of grease.
- **Meringue Cracking**: Small cracks in the meringue are normal. If it cracks too much, it might be due to rapid cooling or baking at too high a temperature.
- **Fruit**: Choose fruit that isn't too juicy to avoid sogginess. Seasonal fruits like berries and kiwis are great choices.

Enjoy your Pavlova! It's a beautiful and delicious dessert that's perfect for special occasions or as a light, refreshing treat.

Cinnamon Rolls

Ingredients

For the Dough:

- 1 cup (240ml) whole milk
- 1/2 cup (115g) unsalted butter, cut into pieces
- 1/4 cup (50g) granulated sugar
- 2 1/4 teaspoons (1 packet) active dry yeast
- 1/4 cup (50g) granulated sugar
- 1/2 teaspoon salt
- 2 large eggs
- 4 cups (500g) all-purpose flour

For the Cinnamon Filling:

- 1/2 cup (115g) unsalted butter, softened
- 1 cup (200g) packed brown sugar
- 2 tablespoons ground cinnamon

For the Cream Cheese Frosting:

- 4 oz (115g) cream cheese, softened
- 1/4 cup (60g) unsalted butter, softened
- 1 1/2 cups (190g) powdered sugar
- 1 teaspoon vanilla extract
- 1-2 tablespoons milk (to achieve desired consistency)

Instructions

1. Prepare the Dough:

1. **Warm Milk**: In a small saucepan, heat the milk until it's warm but not hot (about 110°F/45°C). Remove from heat and add the butter, stirring until melted. Let the mixture cool slightly.
2. **Activate Yeast**: In a large bowl, sprinkle the yeast over the warm milk mixture. Add 1/4 cup (50g) granulated sugar and let it sit for about 5 minutes, or until it becomes frothy.
3. **Mix Dough**: Add the remaining sugar, salt, and eggs to the yeast mixture. Gradually add the flour, mixing until a dough forms.
4. **Knead**: Turn the dough onto a floured surface and knead for about 5-7 minutes, or until the dough is smooth and elastic. You can also use a stand mixer with a dough hook for this process.
5. **First Rise**: Place the dough in a lightly greased bowl, cover with a clean kitchen towel or plastic wrap, and let it rise in a warm place for about 1 hour, or until doubled in size.

2. Prepare the Filling:

1. **Mix Filling**: In a medium bowl, combine the softened butter, brown sugar, and cinnamon until well blended.

3. Shape the Cinnamon Rolls:

1. **Roll Out Dough**: After the dough has risen, punch it down and turn it out onto a lightly floured surface. Roll it out into a rectangle about 16x12 inches (40x30 cm).
2. **Spread Filling**: Evenly spread the cinnamon filling over the dough, leaving a small border around the edges.
3. **Roll Up Dough**: Starting from the long side, tightly roll the dough into a log. Pinch the seam to seal.
4. **Cut Rolls**: Using a sharp knife or dental floss, cut the roll into 12 even pieces. Arrange the rolls in a greased 9x13-inch (23x33 cm) baking dish or two 9-inch (23 cm) round pans.

4. Second Rise:

1. **Let Rise**: Cover the rolls with a clean towel or plastic wrap and let them rise in a warm place for about 30 minutes, or until puffed and doubled in size.

5. Bake:

1. **Preheat Oven**: Preheat your oven to 350°F (175°C).
2. **Bake Rolls**: Bake the cinnamon rolls for 20-25 minutes, or until golden brown. The center should be cooked through and the edges should be nicely browned.

6. Prepare the Frosting:

1. **Mix Frosting**: In a medium bowl, beat the cream cheese and butter until smooth. Gradually add the powdered sugar and vanilla extract, beating until well combined. Add milk 1 tablespoon at a time until the frosting reaches your desired consistency.

7. Frost and Serve:

1. **Cool Slightly**: Allow the cinnamon rolls to cool slightly before frosting.
2. **Frost Rolls**: Spread the cream cheese frosting over the warm rolls.

Tips:

- **Dough Temperature**: Ensure the milk isn't too hot when activating the yeast, as it can kill the yeast.
- **Flour Measurement**: For best results, measure the flour by spooning it into the measuring cup and leveling it off, rather than scooping directly from the bag.

- **Rolling**: Use a rolling pin to get an even thickness for the dough, which helps in uniform baking and filling distribution.

Enjoy your homemade cinnamon rolls! They're perfect for breakfast, brunch, or as a sweet treat with a cup of coffee.

Carrot Cake

Ingredients

For the Carrot Cake:

- 1 1/2 cups (190g) all-purpose flour
- 1 cup (200g) granulated sugar
- 1/2 cup (100g) packed brown sugar
- 1 teaspoon baking powder
- 1/2 teaspoon baking soda
- 1/2 teaspoon salt
- 1 teaspoon ground cinnamon
- 1/2 teaspoon ground nutmeg
- 1/2 teaspoon ground ginger (optional)
- 1/2 cup (120ml) vegetable oil or canola oil
- 3 large eggs
- 2 cups (240g) finely grated carrots (about 4 medium carrots)
- 1/2 cup (80g) crushed pineapple, drained
- 1/2 cup (80g) chopped walnuts or pecans (optional)
- 1/2 cup (75g) raisins (optional)
- 1 teaspoon vanilla extract

For the Cream Cheese Frosting:

- 8 oz (225g) cream cheese, softened
- 1/2 cup (115g) unsalted butter, softened
- 3-4 cups (375-500g) powdered sugar, sifted
- 1 teaspoon vanilla extract

Instructions

1. Prepare the Cake:

1. **Preheat Oven**: Preheat your oven to 350°F (175°C). Grease and flour two 8-inch (20 cm) round cake pans, or line them with parchment paper.
2. **Mix Dry Ingredients**: In a medium bowl, whisk together the flour, granulated sugar, brown sugar, baking powder, baking soda, salt, cinnamon, nutmeg, and ginger.
3. **Mix Wet Ingredients**: In a large bowl, whisk together the oil, eggs, and vanilla extract. Add the grated carrots, crushed pineapple, and mix well.
4. **Combine**: Gradually add the dry ingredients to the wet ingredients, stirring until just combined. Fold in the nuts and raisins if using.
5. **Bake**: Divide the batter evenly between the prepared cake pans. Smooth the tops with a spatula.

6. **Bake**: Bake for 25-30 minutes, or until a toothpick inserted into the center comes out clean. The tops should spring back when lightly touched.

2. Cool the Cake:

1. **Cool in Pans**: Allow the cakes to cool in the pans for 10 minutes, then turn them out onto a wire rack to cool completely before frosting.

3. Prepare the Cream Cheese Frosting:

1. **Beat Cream Cheese and Butter**: In a mixing bowl, beat the softened cream cheese and butter together until smooth and creamy.
2. **Add Powdered Sugar**: Gradually add the powdered sugar, one cup at a time, beating until fully incorporated and smooth.
3. **Add Vanilla**: Beat in the vanilla extract.

4. Frost the Cake:

1. **Frost**: Place one cake layer on a serving plate or cake stand. Spread a layer of frosting on top. Place the second layer on top and frost the top and sides of the cake.
2. **Decorate**: If desired, decorate with additional chopped nuts, grated carrots, or a sprinkle of cinnamon.

Tips:

- **Carrots**: Grate the carrots finely to ensure they blend well into the batter and don't create large chunks.
- **Pineapple**: Make sure to drain the crushed pineapple thoroughly to avoid excess moisture in the cake.
- **Room Temperature**: For the best texture, ensure that the cream cheese and butter are at room temperature before making the frosting.

Enjoy your homemade carrot cake! It's a wonderfully moist and flavorful dessert that's perfect for any occasion, from everyday treats to special celebrations.

Raspberries and Cream Tart

Ingredients

For the Tart Crust:

- 1 1/2 cups (190g) all-purpose flour
- 1/2 cup (100g) granulated sugar
- 1/2 cup (115g) **unsalted butter**, cold and cut into small pieces
- 1/4 teaspoon salt
- 1 large egg yolk
- 1-2 tablespoons ice water (as needed)

For the Cream Filling:

- 1 cup (240ml) heavy cream
- 1/2 cup (120ml) whole milk
- 1/2 cup (100g) granulated sugar
- 3 large egg yolks
- 1 teaspoon vanilla extract
- 2 tablespoons all-purpose flour

For the Topping:

- 2 cups (250g) fresh raspberries
- 1/4 cup (30g) powdered sugar (optional, for dusting)
- **Mint leaves** (for garnish, optional)

Instructions

1. Prepare the Tart Crust:

1. **Preheat Oven**: Preheat your oven to 375°F (190°C).
2. **Mix Dry Ingredients**: In a large bowl, whisk together the flour, granulated sugar, and salt.
3. **Cut in Butter**: Add the cold butter pieces to the flour mixture. Use a pastry cutter or your fingers to work the butter into the flour until the mixture resembles coarse crumbs.
4. **Add Egg Yolk**: Stir in the egg yolk until combined. If the dough is too dry, add ice water, one tablespoon at a time, until it comes together.
5. **Chill Dough**: Gather the dough into a disk, wrap it in plastic wrap, and refrigerate for at least 30 minutes.
6. **Roll Out Dough**: On a lightly floured surface, roll out the dough to fit a 9-inch (23 cm) tart pan. Press the dough into the pan, trimming any excess.

7. **Pre-bake Crust**: Line the crust with parchment paper and fill with pie weights or dried beans. Bake for 15 minutes, then remove the weights and parchment and bake for an additional 5-7 minutes, or until the crust is golden brown. Let it cool completely.

2. Prepare the Cream Filling:

1. **Heat Cream and Milk**: In a medium saucepan, heat the heavy cream and milk over medium heat until it just begins to simmer.
2. **Whisk Egg Yolks and Sugar**: In a separate bowl, whisk together the egg yolks, sugar, and flour until smooth.
3. **Temper Egg Mixture**: Gradually whisk the hot cream mixture into the egg yolk mixture to temper it.
4. **Cook Filling**: Return the mixture to the saucepan and cook over medium heat, whisking constantly, until it thickens and coats the back of a spoon (about 2-3 minutes). Do not let it boil.
5. **Add Vanilla**: Remove from heat and stir in the vanilla extract. Let it cool slightly.

3. Assemble the Tart:

1. **Fill Crust**: Pour the cream filling into the cooled tart crust and smooth the top with a spatula.
2. **Chill**: Refrigerate the tart for at least 2 hours, or until the filling is set.

4. Add Topping:

1. **Top with Raspberries**: Just before serving, arrange the fresh raspberries on top of the tart.
2. **Dust with Powdered Sugar**: Optionally, dust with powdered sugar for a touch of sweetness and elegance.
3. **Garnish**: Garnish with mint leaves if desired.

Tips:

- **Crust**: Make sure to thoroughly chill the crust dough before baking to prevent shrinkage.
- **Filling**: Stir constantly while cooking the cream filling to avoid lumps or curdling.
- **Raspberries**: Use fresh raspberries for the best flavor and texture. If using frozen, thaw and drain them well.

Enjoy your Raspberries and Cream Tart! It's a stunning and delectable dessert that's sure to impress anyone who tastes it.

S'mores Bars

Ingredients

For the Crust:

- **1 1/2 cups (150g) graham cracker crumbs**
- **1/2 cup (100g) granulated sugar**
- **1/2 cup (115g) unsalted butter**, melted

For the Filling:

- **1 cup (200g) semi-sweet chocolate chips**
- **1 cup (200g) milk chocolate chips**
- **1 cup (240ml) sweetened condensed milk**
- **2 cups (200g) mini marshmallows**

Instructions

1. Prepare the Crust:

1. **Preheat Oven**: Preheat your oven to 350°F (175°C). Line an 8x8-inch (20x20 cm) baking dish with parchment paper, leaving some overhang for easy removal later.
2. **Mix Crust Ingredients**: In a medium bowl, combine the graham cracker crumbs, granulated sugar, and melted butter. Mix until the crumbs are evenly coated.
3. **Press Crust**: Press the graham cracker mixture firmly into the bottom of the prepared baking dish to form an even layer.

2. Prepare the Filling:

1. **Melt Chocolate**: In a heatproof bowl, combine the semi-sweet and milk chocolate chips. Add the sweetened condensed milk. Microwave in 30-second intervals, stirring after each interval, until the chocolate is completely melted and smooth. You can also melt the chocolate mixture over a double boiler if preferred.
2. **Add Marshmallows**: Stir in 1 1/2 cups of mini marshmallows into the melted chocolate mixture.

3. Assemble the Bars:

1. **Spread Filling**: Pour the chocolate and marshmallow mixture over the graham cracker crust, spreading it evenly with a spatula.
2. **Add Remaining Marshmallows**: Sprinkle the remaining 1/2 cup of mini marshmallows over the top.

4. Bake:

1. **Bake Bars**: Bake in the preheated oven for 15-20 minutes, or until the marshmallows on top are golden brown and the filling is set. Keep an eye on the bars to ensure the marshmallows do not burn.
2. **Cool Completely**: Allow the bars to cool completely in the pan on a wire rack. For easier cutting, you can refrigerate them for about 1 hour.

5. Cut and Serve:

1. **Cut Bars**: Once cooled, use the parchment paper overhang to lift the bars out of the pan. Cut into squares or rectangles.
2. **Serve**: Enjoy your s'mores bars at room temperature or chilled.

Tips:

- **Crust Firmness**: Make sure to press the graham cracker crust firmly into the pan to prevent it from falling apart when cutting.
- **Chocolate Variations**: You can use all semi-sweet or all milk chocolate chips based on your preference, or try using different types of chocolate.
- **Marshmallow Texture**: If you prefer a more toasted marshmallow flavor, you can use a kitchen torch to lightly toast the marshmallows after baking.

Enjoy your homemade S'mores Bars! They're a perfect treat for parties, picnics, or just as a sweet indulgence.

Creme Caramel

Ingredients

For the Caramel:

- 1 cup (200g) granulated sugar
- 1/4 cup (60ml) water

For the Custard:

- 4 large eggs
- 1 can (14 oz/400ml) sweetened condensed milk
- 1 can (12 oz/355ml) evaporated milk
- 1 cup (240ml) whole milk
- 1 teaspoon vanilla extract

Instructions

1. Prepare the Caramel:

1. **Cook Caramel**: In a medium, heavy-bottomed saucepan, combine the granulated sugar and water. Cook over medium heat, swirling the pan occasionally (do not stir), until the sugar has dissolved and turns a golden amber color. This usually takes about 8-10 minutes.
2. **Pour Caramel**: Immediately pour the caramel into the bottom of your ramekins or custard cups, swirling each to coat the bottom evenly. Be careful, as the caramel will be very hot. Set aside to cool and harden.

2. Prepare the Custard:

1. **Preheat Oven**: Preheat your oven to 325°F (160°C). Prepare a large baking dish or roasting pan that will hold your ramekins or custard cups.
2. **Mix Custard Ingredients**: In a large bowl, whisk together the eggs, sweetened condensed milk, evaporated milk, whole milk, and vanilla extract until well combined.
3. **Strain Mixture**: For a smoother custard, strain the mixture through a fine-mesh sieve into another bowl or large measuring jug.

3. Assemble and Bake:

1. **Fill Ramekins**: Pour the custard mixture evenly into the caramel-coated ramekins or custard cups.
2. **Prepare Water Bath**: Place the filled ramekins into the prepared baking dish or roasting pan. Carefully pour hot water into the baking dish around the ramekins, about halfway up the sides of the ramekins, to create a water bath.

3. **Bake**: Bake in the preheated oven for 45-55 minutes, or until the custard is set and a knife inserted into the center comes out clean. The custard should be firm but still slightly jiggly in the center.

4. Cool and Unmold:

1. **Cool**: Remove the ramekins from the water bath and let them cool to room temperature. Then, refrigerate for at least 4 hours, or preferably overnight, to fully set and chill.
2. **Unmold**: To unmold, run a knife around the edge of each custard to loosen it. Invert a serving plate over the ramekin, then flip the ramekin to release the crème caramel onto the plate. The caramel sauce will flow over the top.

Tips:

- **Caramel Color**: Be careful not to burn the sugar when making the caramel. It should be a deep golden color, but not dark brown.
- **Water Bath**: The water bath helps the custard cook evenly and prevents cracking. Ensure the water level is correct and avoid getting any water into the custards.
- **Straining**: Straining the custard mixture helps remove any egg bits and ensures a smooth texture.

Enjoy your Crème Caramel! It's a sophisticated and delicious dessert that's perfect for finishing off a special meal.

Apple Pie

Ingredients

For the Pie Crust:

- **2 1/2 cups (315g) all-purpose flour**
- **1 cup (225g) unsalted butter**, cold and cut into small pieces
- **1/4 cup (50g) granulated sugar**
- **1/2 teaspoon salt**
- **1/4 cup (60ml) ice water** (more if needed)

For the Apple Filling:

- **6-7 cups (about 1.5kg) peeled, cored, and sliced apples** (such as Granny Smith, Honeycrisp, or a mix)
- **1/2 cup (100g) granulated sugar**
- **1/4 cup (50g) packed brown sugar**
- **1/4 cup (30g) all-purpose flour** (or cornstarch)
- **1 teaspoon ground cinnamon**
- **1/4 teaspoon ground nutmeg**
- **1/4 teaspoon ground allspice** (optional)
- **1 tablespoon lemon juice**
- **1 teaspoon vanilla extract** (optional)

For Assembling:

- **1 large egg**, beaten (for egg wash)
- **1 tablespoon granulated sugar** (for sprinkling on top)

Instructions

1. Prepare the Pie Crust:

1. **Mix Dry Ingredients**: In a large bowl, whisk together the flour, sugar, and salt.
2. **Cut in Butter**: Add the cold butter pieces. Using a pastry cutter or your fingers, cut the butter into the flour mixture until it resembles coarse crumbs with pea-sized pieces.
3. **Add Ice Water**: Gradually add the ice water, one tablespoon at a time, mixing until the dough just begins to come together. You may need a bit more or less water.
4. **Form Dough**: Divide the dough into two equal portions, shape each portion into a disk, wrap in plastic wrap, and refrigerate for at least 1 hour or up to 2 days.

2. Prepare the Apple Filling:

1. **Prepare Apples**: Peel, core, and slice the apples. Place them in a large bowl.

2. **Mix Filling Ingredients**: In a separate bowl, combine the granulated sugar, brown sugar, flour (or cornstarch), cinnamon, nutmeg, allspice (if using), lemon juice, and vanilla extract. Toss the mixture with the sliced apples until they are well coated.

3. Assemble the Pie:

1. **Preheat Oven**: Preheat your oven to 425°F (220°C).
2. **Roll Out Dough**: On a lightly floured surface, roll out one disk of dough to fit a 9-inch (23 cm) pie pan. Gently transfer it to the pan, pressing it into the edges.
3. **Add Filling**: Pour the apple filling into the prepared crust, spreading it evenly.
4. **Top Crust**: Roll out the second disk of dough and place it over the filling. You can create a lattice top by cutting the dough into strips and weaving them over the filling, or simply cover with the whole rolled dough.
5. **Seal Edges**: Trim any excess dough, then crimp the edges to seal. Cut a few small slits in the top crust to allow steam to escape. Brush the top with the beaten egg and sprinkle with granulated sugar.

4. Bake the Pie:

1. **Bake**: Bake in the preheated oven for 45-55 minutes, or until the crust is golden brown and the filling is bubbling. If the edges of the crust start to brown too quickly, cover them with aluminum foil.
2. **Cool**: Allow the pie to cool on a wire rack for at least 2 hours before serving. This helps the filling set and makes it easier to slice.

Tips:

- **Apple Selection**: Use a mix of tart and sweet apples for the best flavor and texture.
- **Crust Handling**: Keep the dough cold to ensure a flaky crust. If it becomes too warm while working, refrigerate it briefly before continuing.
- **Filling Thickness**: If the filling seems too dry, you can add a little extra lemon juice or a splash of water.

Enjoy your homemade apple pie! It's a comforting and delicious dessert that's perfect for any occasion, from casual family dinners to holiday celebrations.

Pear Almond Tart

Ingredients

For the Tart Crust:

- **1 1/2 cups (190g) all-purpose flour**
- **1/4 cup (50g) granulated sugar**
- **1/2 teaspoon salt**
- **1/2 cup (115g) unsalted butter**, cold and cut into small pieces
- **1 large egg yolk**
- **1-2 tablespoons ice water**

For the Almond Filling:

- **1/2 cup (115g) unsalted butter**, softened
- **1/2 cup (100g) granulated sugar**
- **1 cup (100g) almond meal** (or finely ground almonds)
- **2 large eggs**
- **1 teaspoon vanilla extract**
- **1 tablespoon all-purpose flour**

For the Pears:

- **3-4 ripe pears** (such as Bosc or Anjou), peeled, cored, and sliced thinly
- **1 tablespoon lemon juice** (to prevent browning)

For Garnish:

- **Powdered sugar** (optional, for dusting)
- **Sliced almonds** (optional, for topping)

Instructions

1. Prepare the Tart Crust:

1. **Preheat Oven**: Preheat your oven to 350°F (175°C). Grease a 9-inch (23 cm) tart pan with a removable bottom.
2. **Mix Dry Ingredients**: In a large bowl, whisk together the flour, granulated sugar, and salt.
3. **Cut in Butter**: Add the cold butter pieces to the flour mixture. Use a pastry cutter or your fingers to work the butter into the flour until the mixture resembles coarse crumbs.
4. **Add Egg Yolk**: Stir in the egg yolk until combined. If the dough is too dry, add ice water, one tablespoon at a time, until it comes together.
5. **Chill Dough**: Gather the dough into a disk, wrap it in plastic wrap, and refrigerate for at least 30 minutes.

6. **Roll Out Dough**: On a lightly floured surface, roll out the dough to fit the tart pan. Press the dough into the pan, trimming any excess. Chill for another 10 minutes.
7. **Blind Bake**: Line the crust with parchment paper and fill with pie weights or dried beans. Bake for 15 minutes. Remove the weights and parchment and bake for an additional 5 minutes until lightly golden. Set aside to cool.

2. Prepare the Almond Filling:

1. **Cream Butter and Sugar**: In a medium bowl, beat the softened butter and granulated sugar until light and fluffy.
2. **Add Almond Meal**: Mix in the almond meal until well combined.
3. **Add Eggs and Vanilla**: Beat in the eggs one at a time, followed by the vanilla extract.
4. **Add Flour**: Stir in the flour until smooth.

3. Assemble the Tart:

1. **Prepare Pears**: Toss the pear slices with lemon juice to prevent browning.
2. **Fill Tart Shell**: Spread the almond filling evenly over the pre-baked tart crust.
3. **Arrange Pears**: Arrange the pear slices in a decorative pattern on top of the almond filling.

4. Bake the Tart:

1. **Bake**: Bake in the preheated oven for 35-40 minutes, or until the almond filling is set and golden brown, and the pears are tender.
2. **Cool**: Allow the tart to cool completely on a wire rack before removing it from the pan.

5. Garnish and Serve:

1. **Garnish**: Dust with powdered sugar and sprinkle with sliced almonds if desired.
2. **Serve**: Serve at room temperature or slightly warmed.

Tips:

- **Pear Selection**: Choose firm but ripe pears to ensure they hold their shape during baking.
- **Tart Pan**: Using a tart pan with a removable bottom makes it easier to remove the tart without breaking it.
- **Almond Meal**: If you can't find almond meal, you can make your own by grinding blanched almonds in a food processor until finely ground.

Enjoy your Pear Almond Tart! It's a sophisticated dessert that pairs beautifully with a cup of tea or coffee.

Chocolate Soufflé

Ingredients

For the Soufflé:

- **2 tablespoons (30g) unsalted butter**, plus extra for greasing
- **1/4 cup (50g) granulated sugar**, plus extra for coating
- **3 ounces (85g) bittersweet or semisweet chocolate**, chopped
- **1 tablespoon (15ml) milk**
- **2 large egg yolks**
- **1 teaspoon vanilla extract**
- **4 large egg whites**
- **1/4 teaspoon cream of tartar**
- **1/4 cup (50g) granulated sugar** (for the egg whites)

Instructions

1. Prepare the Ramekins:

1. **Preheat Oven**: Preheat your oven to 375°F (190°C). Place a rack in the center of the oven.
2. **Grease Ramekins**: Generously butter the insides of four 6-ounce (180ml) ramekins. Make sure to coat the sides well to help the soufflé rise evenly.
3. **Sugar Ramekins**: Sprinkle a bit of granulated sugar into each ramekin, tapping them gently to coat the inside evenly. Tap out any excess sugar.

2. Make the Chocolate Base:

1. **Melt Chocolate**: In a heatproof bowl over a pot of simmering water (double boiler method), melt the chopped chocolate with the milk, stirring until smooth. You can also melt the chocolate in the microwave in 30-second intervals, stirring after each interval.
2. **Add Egg Yolks**: Remove the bowl from heat. Stir in the egg yolks and vanilla extract until fully combined and smooth.

3. Prepare the Egg Whites:

1. **Beat Egg Whites**: In a clean, dry bowl, beat the egg whites and cream of tartar using an electric mixer on medium speed until foamy. Gradually add 1/4 cup (50g) of granulated sugar while continuing to beat until stiff, glossy peaks form.
2. **Fold Egg Whites**: Gently fold a small amount of the beaten egg whites into the chocolate mixture to lighten it. Then fold in the remaining egg whites in two additions, being careful not to deflate the mixture.

4. Assemble and Bake:

1. **Fill Ramekins**: Spoon the soufflé mixture evenly into the prepared ramekins, filling each almost to the top. Run your thumb or a small knife around the inside edge of each ramekin to help the soufflés rise evenly.
2. **Bake**: Place the ramekins on a baking sheet and bake in the preheated oven for 12-15 minutes, or until the soufflés are puffed and the tops are set. They should still be slightly soft in the center.

5. Serve:

1. **Serve Immediately**: Soufflés are best served immediately after baking, as they will start to deflate quickly. Dust with powdered sugar if desired.

Tips:

- **Room Temperature Ingredients**: Ensure all ingredients are at room temperature for best results.
- **Egg Whites**: Make sure your mixing bowl and beaters are completely clean and dry when whipping the egg whites. Any grease or moisture can prevent them from whipping properly.
- **Baking Time**: Oven temperatures can vary, so start checking the soufflés a minute or two before the recommended baking time to avoid overcooking.

Enjoy your Chocolate Soufflé! It's a wonderfully indulgent and impressive dessert that's sure to delight chocolate lovers.

Vanilla Pudding

Ingredients

- 2 3/4 cups (680ml) whole milk
- 1/2 cup (100g) granulated sugar
- 1/4 cup (30g) cornstarch
- 1/4 teaspoon salt
- 3 large egg yolks
- 2 tablespoons (30g) unsalted butter
- 2 teaspoons vanilla extract

Instructions

1. Prepare the Ingredients:

1. **Mix Dry Ingredients**: In a medium saucepan, whisk together the sugar, cornstarch, and salt.
2. **Heat Milk**: Gradually whisk in the milk until the mixture is smooth and well combined.

2. Cook the Pudding:

1. **Heat Mixture**: Place the saucepan over medium heat. Cook the mixture, stirring constantly, until it starts to thicken and begins to bubble (about 5-7 minutes). Make sure to scrape the bottom and sides of the pan to prevent the mixture from sticking or burning.
2. **Temper Egg Yolks**: In a separate bowl, whisk the egg yolks. Gradually whisk in about 1/2 cup of the hot milk mixture to temper the yolks.
3. **Combine Mixtures**: Return the egg yolk mixture to the saucepan, whisking constantly. Continue to cook and stir until the pudding thickens further (about 1-2 more minutes).

3. Finish and Chill:

1. **Add Butter and Vanilla**: Remove the saucepan from heat. Stir in the butter and vanilla extract until the butter is fully melted and the pudding is smooth.
2. **Cool**: Pour the pudding into individual serving dishes or a large bowl. To prevent a skin from forming, place a piece of plastic wrap directly on the surface of the pudding.
3. **Chill**: Refrigerate for at least 2 hours, or until set and cold.

4. Serve:

1. **Serve**: Serve chilled, plain or with toppings like whipped cream, fresh fruit, or a sprinkle of cinnamon.

Tips:

- **Constant Stirring**: Constant stirring helps prevent lumps and ensures an even consistency.
- **Cornstarch Mixture**: Make sure the cornstarch is fully dissolved in the milk before heating to avoid lumps.
- **Egg Yolks**: Tempering the egg yolks helps to avoid curdling. Make sure to whisk the yolks slowly into the hot mixture and not the other way around.

Enjoy your homemade vanilla pudding! It's a comforting and versatile dessert that pairs well with a variety of toppings and can be enjoyed on its own.

Strawberry Rhubarb Crisp

Ingredients

For the Filling:

- **2 cups (300g) fresh strawberries**, hulled and sliced
- **2 cups (300g) fresh rhubarb**, chopped into 1/2-inch pieces
- **1 cup (200g) granulated sugar**
- **2 tablespoons cornstarch**
- **1 tablespoon lemon juice**
- **1/2 teaspoon vanilla extract**

For the Crisp Topping:

- **1 cup (90g) old-fashioned rolled oats**
- **1/2 cup (65g) all-purpose flour**
- **1/2 cup (100g) brown sugar**, packed
- **1/2 teaspoon ground cinnamon**
- **1/4 teaspoon salt**
- **1/2 cup (115g) unsalted butter**, cold and cut into small pieces

Instructions

1. Prepare the Filling:

1. **Preheat Oven**: Preheat your oven to 350°F (175°C). Grease a 9x9-inch (23x23 cm) baking dish or a similar-sized dish.
2. **Mix Filling Ingredients**: In a large bowl, combine the strawberries, rhubarb, granulated sugar, cornstarch, lemon juice, and vanilla extract. Toss until the fruit is evenly coated with the sugar and cornstarch mixture.
3. **Transfer to Dish**: Pour the fruit mixture into the prepared baking dish and spread it evenly.

2. Prepare the Crisp Topping:

1. **Mix Dry Ingredients**: In a medium bowl, combine the rolled oats, flour, brown sugar, cinnamon, and salt.
2. **Cut in Butter**: Add the cold butter pieces to the dry ingredients. Using a pastry cutter, fork, or your fingers, cut the butter into the mixture until it resembles coarse crumbs with pea-sized pieces.
3. **Top Fruit Mixture**: Sprinkle the crisp topping evenly over the fruit filling in the baking dish.

3. Bake:

1. **Bake Crisp**: Bake in the preheated oven for 45-55 minutes, or until the topping is golden brown and the fruit is bubbly and tender. You may need to cover the crisp with aluminum foil if the topping starts to brown too quickly.

4. Serve:

1. **Cool**: Let the crisp cool slightly before serving. This allows the juices to thicken up a bit.
2. **Serve**: Serve warm or at room temperature. It's delicious on its own or with a scoop of vanilla ice cream or a dollop of whipped cream.

Tips:

- **Fruit Freshness**: Make sure to use fresh, firm strawberries and rhubarb for the best texture and flavor. Frozen fruit can be used but may release more liquid, so adjust the cornstarch as needed.
- **Topping Texture**: For an extra crunchy topping, you can add chopped nuts (like almonds or pecans) to the topping mixture.
- **Avoid Soggy Crisp**: If you find that the fruit has released a lot of juice during baking, you can cook the crisp for a few more minutes to help thicken the filling.

Enjoy your Strawberry Rhubarb Crisp! It's a perfect combination of sweet and tart flavors with a satisfying crunch.

Hazelnut Meringue Cake

Ingredients

For the Meringue Layers:

- **1 1/2 cups (150g) hazelnuts**, toasted and finely ground
- **6 large egg whites**, at room temperature
- **1 1/2 cups (300g) granulated sugar**
- **1/4 teaspoon cream of tartar**
- **1/2 teaspoon vanilla extract**

For the Filling:

- **1 cup (240ml) heavy cream**
- **1/2 cup (100g) granulated sugar**
- **1 teaspoon vanilla extract**
- **1/2 cup (120g) unsalted butter**, softened
- **1/2 cup (120g) hazelnut spread** (such as Nutella)
- **1/2 cup (120g) finely chopped toasted hazelnuts** (for garnish)

Instructions

1. Prepare the Meringue Layers:

1. **Preheat Oven**: Preheat your oven to 275°F (135°C). Line two baking sheets with parchment paper.
2. **Prepare Hazelnuts**: Toast the hazelnuts in the oven for about 10 minutes until they are fragrant and their skins are slightly cracked. Let them cool, then rub off the skins and finely grind the nuts in a food processor. Set aside.
3. **Beat Egg Whites**: In a clean, dry mixing bowl, beat the egg whites and cream of tartar using an electric mixer on medium speed until foamy.
4. **Add Sugar**: Gradually add the granulated sugar, about 1 tablespoon at a time, while continuing to beat on high speed until stiff, glossy peaks form. The meringue should be smooth and shiny.
5. **Add Hazelnuts and Vanilla**: Gently fold the ground hazelnuts and vanilla extract into the meringue mixture.
6. **Shape Meringues**: Divide the meringue mixture between the two prepared baking sheets and spread it into two even circles or rectangles, depending on your preference. Smooth the tops with a spatula.
7. **Bake**: Bake in the preheated oven for 1 to 1 1/2 hours, or until the meringue layers are crisp and dry. They should come off the parchment easily. Let them cool completely on a wire rack.

2. Prepare the Filling:

1. **Whip Cream**: In a medium bowl, whip the heavy cream with the granulated sugar and vanilla extract until soft peaks form.
2. **Mix Butter and Hazelnut Spread**: In another bowl, beat the softened butter and hazelnut spread until smooth and well combined.
3. **Combine**: Gently fold the whipped cream into the butter and hazelnut spread mixture until fully combined.

3. Assemble the Cake:

1. **Layer Meringues**: Place one meringue layer on a serving plate or cake stand. Spread half of the filling over the meringue.
2. **Add Second Layer**: Top with the second meringue layer and spread the remaining filling on top.
3. **Garnish**: Sprinkle the finely chopped toasted hazelnuts over the top of the cake for garnish.

4. Serve:

1. **Serve**: The cake is best served shortly after assembling. It's a beautiful dessert with a crunchy meringue texture and creamy, nutty filling.

Tips:

- **Meringue Texture**: Make sure your mixing bowl and beaters are completely clean and dry when whipping the egg whites. Even a small amount of grease can prevent the meringue from reaching stiff peaks.
- **Hazelnuts**: Toast the hazelnuts to enhance their flavor and make them easier to grind. Be sure to cool them completely before processing.
- **Meringue Baking**: If the meringues are still soft in the center after baking, continue baking with the oven turned off and the door slightly ajar until they are completely dry.

Enjoy your Hazelnut Meringue Cake! It's a rich and delightful dessert that's perfect for impressing your guests or for a special treat.

Key Lime Cheesecake

Ingredients

For the Crust:

- 1 1/2 cups (150g) graham cracker crumbs
- 1/4 cup (50g) granulated sugar
- 1/2 cup (115g) unsalted butter, melted

For the Filling:

- 3 (8-ounce/225g each) packages cream cheese, softened
- 1 cup (200g) granulated sugar
- 3 large eggs
- 1 cup (240ml) sour cream
- 1/2 cup (120ml) fresh Key lime juice (or regular lime juice)
- 2 teaspoons lime zest
- 1 teaspoon vanilla extract

For the Topping:

- 1 cup (240ml) heavy cream
- 2 tablespoons powdered sugar
- 1 teaspoon vanilla extract
- Key lime slices or zest, for garnish

Instructions

1. Prepare the Crust:

1. **Preheat Oven**: Preheat your oven to 325°F (160°C).
2. **Mix Crust Ingredients**: In a medium bowl, combine the graham cracker crumbs, granulated sugar, and melted butter. Mix until the crumbs are evenly coated.
3. **Press Crust**: Press the mixture firmly into the bottom of a 9-inch (23 cm) springform pan to form an even layer.
4. **Bake Crust**: Bake in the preheated oven for 8-10 minutes, or until lightly golden. Remove from the oven and let it cool while you prepare the filling.

2. Prepare the Filling:

1. **Beat Cream Cheese**: In a large mixing bowl, beat the softened cream cheese with an electric mixer until smooth and creamy.
2. **Add Sugar**: Gradually add the granulated sugar, beating until well combined.
3. **Add Eggs**: Add the eggs one at a time, beating on low speed after each addition until just combined.

4. **Mix in Remaining Ingredients**: Add the sour cream, Key lime juice, lime zest, and vanilla extract. Beat until smooth and fully incorporated.
5. **Pour Filling**: Pour the cheesecake filling over the prepared crust in the springform pan and smooth the top with a spatula.

3. Bake the Cheesecake:

1. **Prepare Water Bath**: To prevent cracking, place the springform pan in a larger roasting pan. Fill the roasting pan with hot water until it comes halfway up the sides of the springform pan.
2. **Bake**: Bake in the preheated oven for 55-65 minutes, or until the center is set but slightly jiggly. The edges should be firm and the center should not be completely firm when you gently shake the pan.
3. **Cool**: Turn off the oven and crack the oven door slightly. Let the cheesecake cool in the oven for 1 hour. Remove from the oven and refrigerate for at least 4 hours, preferably overnight.

4. Prepare the Topping:

1. **Whip Cream**: In a medium bowl, whip the heavy cream, powdered sugar, and vanilla extract using an electric mixer until soft peaks form.
2. **Top Cheesecake**: Spread the whipped cream over the chilled cheesecake, or pipe it in decorative patterns if you prefer.

5. Garnish and Serve:

1. **Garnish**: Garnish with Key lime slices or additional lime zest if desired.
2. **Serve**: Slice and serve chilled.

Tips:

- **Cream Cheese**: Ensure the cream cheese is softened to room temperature for a smooth filling.
- **Water Bath**: Using a water bath helps to prevent cracks in the cheesecake by providing a more even baking environment.
- **Chilling Time**: Allowing the cheesecake to chill overnight helps the flavors to develop and makes it easier to slice.

Enjoy your Key Lime Cheesecake! It's a refreshing and indulgent dessert that combines the best of both cheesecake and Key lime pie.

Molten Chocolate Mug Cake

Ingredients

- 4 tablespoons (55g) unsalted butter
- 1/4 cup (50g) granulated sugar
- 1/4 cup (50g) packed brown sugar
- 1/4 cup (30g) unsweetened cocoa powder
- 1/4 teaspoon baking powder
- Pinch of salt
- 1 large egg
- 1/4 teaspoon vanilla extract
- 1/4 cup (30g) all-purpose flour
- 2 tablespoons (30g) chocolate chips or chopped chocolate

Instructions

1. Melt Butter:

1. **Melt Butter**: In a microwave-safe mug, melt the butter in the microwave in 20-30 second intervals, stirring in between, until completely melted.

2. Mix Ingredients:

1. **Combine Sugars and Cocoa**: To the melted butter, add the granulated sugar, brown sugar, cocoa powder, baking powder, and salt. Stir until well combined.
2. **Add Egg and Vanilla**: Add the egg and vanilla extract to the mixture, stirring until smooth.
3. **Incorporate Flour**: Add the flour and mix until just combined. Be careful not to overmix.
4. **Add Chocolate Chips**: Fold in the chocolate chips or chopped chocolate.

3. Cook Mug Cake:

1. **Microwave**: Microwave the mug on high for 1 minute to 1 minute and 15 seconds. The cake should rise and appear set around the edges but still slightly gooey in the center. Cooking times may vary depending on the wattage of your microwave.
2. **Check Doneness**: If needed, continue microwaving in 10-second intervals until the cake is cooked to your preference.

4. Serve:

1. **Cool Slightly**: Let the mug cake cool for a few minutes before eating. It will be very hot when first out of the microwave.
2. **Enjoy**: You can enjoy the cake straight from the mug or top it with a scoop of vanilla ice cream, whipped cream, or a drizzle of chocolate sauce if desired.

Tips:

- **Microwave Power**: Adjust the cooking time based on the power of your microwave. Start with 1 minute and increase in 10-second intervals if needed.
- **Mix-Ins**: Feel free to add nuts, caramel bits, or a dollop of peanut butter for extra flavor.
- **Consistency**: The cake should be set around the edges but still soft and gooey in the center for that molten effect.

Enjoy your Molten Chocolate Mug Cake! It's a delightful and easy dessert that's perfect for a quick treat or satisfying a sweet tooth.

Tiramisu Cupcakes

Ingredients

For the Cupcakes:

- 1 1/2 cups (190g) all-purpose flour
- 1 1/2 teaspoons baking powder
- 1/4 teaspoon salt
- 1/2 cup (115g) unsalted butter, softened
- 1 cup (200g) granulated sugar
- 2 large eggs
- 1/2 cup (120ml) whole milk
- 1/2 cup (120ml) strong brewed coffee, cooled
- 1 teaspoon vanilla extract

For the Coffee Soak:

- 1/4 cup (60ml) strong brewed coffee, cooled
- 2 tablespoons (25g) granulated sugar

For the Mascarpone Frosting:

- 8 ounces (225g) mascarpone cheese, softened
- 1 cup (240ml) heavy cream
- 1/2 cup (60g) powdered sugar
- 1 teaspoon vanilla extract
- Cocoa powder, for dusting

Instructions

1. Prepare the Cupcakes:

1. **Preheat Oven**: Preheat your oven to 350°F (175°C). Line a muffin tin with paper liners.
2. **Mix Dry Ingredients**: In a medium bowl, whisk together the flour, baking powder, and salt.
3. **Cream Butter and Sugar**: In a large mixing bowl, beat the softened butter and granulated sugar until light and fluffy.
4. **Add Eggs and Vanilla**: Beat in the eggs one at a time, followed by the vanilla extract.
5. **Combine Wet and Dry Ingredients**: Gradually add the flour mixture to the butter mixture, alternating with the milk, beginning and ending with the flour mixture. Mix until just combined.
6. **Add Coffee**: Stir in the cooled brewed coffee until fully incorporated.

7. **Fill and Bake**: Divide the batter evenly among the cupcake liners, filling each about 2/3 full. Bake for 18-20 minutes, or until a toothpick inserted into the center comes out clean. Let the cupcakes cool completely on a wire rack.

2. Prepare the Coffee Soak:

1. **Combine Coffee and Sugar**: In a small bowl, mix the cooled brewed coffee with the granulated sugar until the sugar is dissolved.

3. Prepare the Mascarpone Frosting:

1. **Beat Mascarpone**: In a large bowl, beat the mascarpone cheese until smooth.
2. **Whip Cream**: In another bowl, whip the heavy cream, powdered sugar, and vanilla extract until stiff peaks form.
3. **Combine**: Gently fold the whipped cream into the mascarpone cheese until smooth and well combined.

4. Assemble the Cupcakes:

1. **Soak Cupcakes**: Using a toothpick or skewer, poke a few holes in the top of each cooled cupcake. Brush or spoon the coffee soak over the cupcakes, allowing it to soak in.
2. **Frost**: Pipe or spread the mascarpone frosting onto the coffee-soaked cupcakes.
3. **Dust with Cocoa**: Lightly dust the tops of the frosted cupcakes with cocoa powder.

5. Serve:

1. **Chill**: For the best flavor, refrigerate the cupcakes for at least 30 minutes before serving to allow the flavors to meld.
2. **Enjoy**: Serve chilled and enjoy the delightful tiramisu flavors in a convenient cupcake form!

Tips:

- **Coffee Strength**: Use strong brewed coffee to ensure the coffee flavor comes through. You can use espresso for an even bolder flavor.
- **Mascarpone Frosting**: Make sure the mascarpone cheese is well-softened for a smooth frosting. Be careful not to overmix the frosting once the whipped cream is added, as it can become too soft.
- **Cupcake Freshness**: These cupcakes are best enjoyed within a few days of baking, as the coffee soak can make them moist over time.

Enjoy your Tiramisu Cupcakes! They're a wonderful blend of classic tiramisu flavors in a fun, individual-sized treat.

Banana Foster

Ingredients

- **4 large ripe bananas**, peeled and sliced into 1/2-inch (1.3 cm) rounds
- **1/4 cup (55g) unsalted butter**
- **1/2 cup (100g) packed brown sugar**
- **1/4 cup (60ml) dark rum** (or light rum if preferred)
- **1/2 teaspoon ground cinnamon**
- **1/4 teaspoon vanilla extract**
- **Vanilla ice cream**, for serving

Instructions

1. Prepare the Bananas:

1. **Slice Bananas**: Peel the bananas and slice them into 1/2-inch (1.3 cm) rounds.

2. Cook the Sauce:

1. **Melt Butter**: In a large skillet or sauté pan, melt the butter over medium heat.
2. **Add Brown Sugar**: Add the brown sugar to the melted butter, stirring until it dissolves and starts to bubble.
3. **Add Cinnamon and Vanilla**: Stir in the ground cinnamon and vanilla extract.

3. Add Bananas:

1. **Cook Bananas**: Add the banana slices to the skillet. Cook for 1-2 minutes, gently stirring, until the bananas are softened and coated in the sauce.

4. Flambé (Optional):

1. **Add Rum**: Carefully pour the dark rum over the bananas.
2. **Flambé**: If you want to flambé the bananas (light the rum on fire), use a long lighter or match. Stand back and ignite the rum. Let the flames subside as the alcohol burns off. This step is optional but adds a dramatic touch.

5. Serve:

1. **Spoon Over Ice Cream**: Serve the warm banana foster over scoops of vanilla ice cream.
2. **Garnish (Optional)**: Garnish with a sprinkle of extra cinnamon or some chopped nuts if desired.

Tips:

- **Flambéing Safety**: If flambéing, ensure you're doing it in a safe environment. Keep a lid or fire extinguisher nearby just in case.
- **Banana Ripeness**: Use ripe but not overly soft bananas to ensure they hold their shape and have a good texture.
- **Rum Substitutes**: If you prefer not to use alcohol, you can skip the flambéing step and just use the rum to add flavor without igniting it.

Enjoy your Banana Foster! It's a rich, flavorful dessert that combines the caramelized sweetness of bananas with the creamy texture of vanilla ice cream.

www.ingramcontent.com/pod-product-compliance
Lightning Source LLC
LaVergne TN
LVHW081600060526
838201LV00054B/1982